The Munchkins of Oz: Legends, Myths, and Realities

Stephen Hoover

The Munchkins of Oz: Legends, Myths, and Realities

Library of Congress Control Number: 2014904036

Copyright © 2013 by Stephen Hoover

Book design by: Cat Stewart

Cover design by: Michael Kraxenberger

ISBN: 978-1-941084-24-3

Contents

Intro

In total, 124 little people showed up in California in 1938 to participate in the filming of a movie that would become a legend; *The Wizard of Oz*. Moderately successful after its first release and more so after the second, the film would go onto become truly famous after it started airing on television during the 1950s.

The little people who played the Munchkins came from all over the nation and from a diverse set of backgrounds. Many came from Europe. Most look back to their time on the set fondly, but, afterwards, there were plenty of unfair and untrue stories spread about them and their time working on the film.

This first part of this book will tell the story of the Munchkins in their own words and as gathered from research. There's a lot to learn about these actors, as well as how their appearances in a fantasy world contributed to changes in the real world.

The second part of the book goes into more detail about the universe that L. Frank Baum created in his children's book, *The Wonderful Wizard of Oz;* including its impact and some of the movies that have built on that universe to great effect. These stories are powerful and wide-ranging. Films based on Baum's work can still pack theaters, well over 100 years after the first story was published.

Chapter 1

The Basics of Oz

When *The Wizard of Oz* was released in 1939, it was the pinnacle of filmmaking. A fantasy adventure of impressive size and scope, the special effects, creative use of color and black and white and, most importantly, the memorable characters, made this film an instant classic.

Among the most memorable characters in *The Wizard of Oz* were the Munchkins. The Munchkins appear near the beginning of the film, just after Dorothy's house falls on the Wicked Witch of the East. The Munchkins proclaim the witch dead and subsequently welcome Dorothy, celebrating her as a hero who will be entered into their Hall of Fame.

When Dorothy gets her mission to follow the Yellow Brick Road, it's the Munchkins who sing her off, launching into one of the film's most distinctive and remembered songs.

Behind all of this is a fascinating story. The incredible complexity of the production meant that, for roughly 10 minutes of screen time, the actors and actresses, crew and everyone else involved in the production spent nearly two months shooting the Munchkin sequence alone. Under these demanding conditions, the actors and actresses suffered indignities not entirely connected to the scope or quality of their work, but due to common attitudes toward little people at the time.

A Story of Painful Prejudices

While much of the information and many of the memories in this book are inherently positive—this film is among the most beloved in the world, after all—there is a great deal of pain, as well. At the time that *The Wizard of Oz* was filmed, society was not particularly fair toward little people, to say the least.

For example, Jerry Maren is probably best remembered as the Munchkin who presents Dorothy with a lollipop as the Munchkins humbly welcome her. He studied performance from a young age and went on to have an impressive career after *The Wizard of Oz*. According to Maren, however, the actors and actresses who played the Munchkins got paid less than Toto the dog. For Toto, the production company paid $125 per week. The little people who played the Munchkins received a comparatively paltry salary of $50 per week. The film was notorious for the very intense working conditions, with the entire cast putting in six-day workweeks and enduring demanding makeup and costuming requirements each day.

There were still other difficulties that the little people working on the film had to endure. Many of the actors and actresses that got the Munchkin roles had a great deal of experience as performers already, with a significant number of them coming from vaudeville and circus work. In fact, like many hardworking travelling performers, some of the little people who worked on the film had a reputation for hard partying that became the stuff of legend.

Despite the fact that the little people who worked on the film were, to a significant extent, accomplished in their trades, they were oftentimes treated as children. In a *People* magazine article from 1989, Meinhardt Raabe, who played the coroner who pronounced the Wicked Witch of the East dead, said that the attitude toward little people at the time was that their small bodies indicated that they had small minds too, and unfortunately, they were sometimes treated as children.

These indignities were oftentimes ones that would likely be considered outrageous today. For instance, Jack Dawn, one of the makeup artists on the film, noted in a *Daily Mail* interview that the little people did not care for being picked up and placed in their makeup chairs. For a modern person, the idea of picking up an actor such as Peter Dinklage of *Game of Thrones* fame and sitting him in his chair like a child would likely cause an instinctive cringe. In the Depression Era, and the years preceding it, during which many of these little people actors had learned their craft, such treatment was not uncommon; nor was it outrageous.

Even today, little people actors sometimes end up turning down roles because, despite society's views on little people having come a long way since the age of *The Wizard of Oz*, they sometimes end up auditioning for roles and finding out that they're insulting or derogatory toward little people. One of today's most notable actors who is also a little person, Danny Woodburn, has turned down roles due to scripts referring to little people as "midgets."

While there are many positive stories that follow in this book, there is also a lot of struggle and pain involved in the lives of actors and actresses who looked different than the norm, particularly during an era not noted for its sensitivity. Despite this, some of the little people who played in *The Wizard of Oz* went on to have very impressive careers and, of course, they remained stars among the rather large following that this film has garnered over the years.

The End of an Era

While *The Wizard of Oz* has lived on as a cultural icon, the people who made the film come alive, including the Munchkins, have largely passed on. Today, there is only one surviving member of the original cast of little people who sincerely delighted audiences when the film was first released. Jerry Maren is the only remaining actor from that portion of the cast. Born in 1920, Maren ended up having a career that spanned the entire 20th century. He worked as an actor in costume, would sometimes stand in for child actors in other roles, and he appeared in several films and documentaries related to *The Wizard of Oz*. Maren also appeared in the comedy television series

Seinfeld and in the Mel Brooks comedy *Spaceballs,* though he was not credited in the film. His extensive filmography reveals a hard-working actor who has far more than one memorable role to his credit, in any regard.

In total, there were 124 little people who took jobs as Munchkins on the set of *The Wizard of Oz.* None of them, except for Maren, are with us any longer today, but their mark on Hollywood is certainly a significant one and the stories of the actors and actresses from the production that went on to notable careers are included in this book.

While the Munchkins may be among the most memorable groups of characters from *The Wizard of Oz,* little people weren't always hired to fill these roles in later productions. In *The Wiz,* for example, a 1978 retelling of the L. Frank Baum novel that featured an African-American cast, the Munchkin parts went to child actors rather than to little people.

While films may have improved their treatment of little people over the years, this book does deal with the past and, because of that, some clarification is necessary.

The Language and Attitudes of the Past

A range of conditions can cause diminished size in human beings, with the most common cause being achondroplasia, which causes a characteristic build with arms and legs that are proportionally shorter than the norm, and a distinctively shorter stature. Some people with dwarfism are proportioned typically for human beings, a condition that's oftentimes referred to as proportionate dwarfism.

In this book, because some of the material is drawn from the past, terms such as "midget" show up. Despite this term still being in common usage, it derives from the era when "freak shows" were popular, according to Little People of America. The preferred and respectful term for anyone under 4'10" in height as an adult is "little person" and that term is used exclusively throughout this book, excepting those occasions where older, more offensive terms are used in the context of quotes or narratives where they were also the terms used by the original speaker and/or writer. The term "midget" is almost universally regarded as offensive and disparaging toward little people.

As the LPA site points out, most people with any form of dwarfism prefer to be referred to by their own names, just as does any other human being, but the term little people is used here when actors and actresses who played the parts of Munchkins are being discussed collectively or as a collective term for people who have an adult size that is below average as a result of one of the conditions that cause dwarfism in human beings.

Enduring in the Modern Era

Despite the fact that *The Wizard of Oz* was made far closer to the year 1900 than it was to the year 2000, the fame of the film and the Munchkins have endured. The Munchkins received a collective star on the Hollywood Walk of Fame in 2007. There were still seven Munchkin performers alive at the time to see the dedication of the monument, some of whom made cross-country journeys just to see the ceremony take place.

The film *The Wizard of Oz* retains a significant fandom around the world. Books, films, magazines, conventions and endless merchandise are still produced that are tied into the film. Films such as *We're Off to See the Munchkins* focused on the experience of the actors and actresses who answered the casting calls for the Munchkin parts and who, upon landing those roles, went on to become part of a production that became film legend.

Interestingly, though this film was based on a book that was full of symbolism related to economics and politics—Oz refers to an ounce, the measure of gold; the ruby slippers were originally silver—it has become one of the most beloved fantasies in the world. A central part of that fantasy are the Munchkins, whose colorful village and warm embrace of Dorothy set the stage for her to go off on her dreamlike adventure—and sometimes nightmare—through a magical world. While the world may have been a much harsher, crueler and unfair place for the actors and actresses that played those Munchkins than it is today, there is also a great deal of hope here. With the exception of one survivor, the entire cast of Munchkins is gone.

Despite that, the Munchkins remain a central element of the entire film and one of its most distinctive ones at that. Their small stature and colorful costumes gave them an appearance that made them easy for children to readily relate to. The sophistication of the production and the fact that their roles in the film were, essentially, as magical creatures allows that scene to be fully fantasy; a wonderful escapism from how little people were oftentimes treated harshly in those days.

Over the years, little people have been given greater acceptance and respect and have not been subjected to so many dehumanizing portrayals in film and television, as was, unfortunately, far too common in the past. It's undeniable that the Munchkins of Oz were influential in this change in attitudes. Like Dorothy's journey, however, little people have endured a long road that has, at times, been much darker than it has been promising. Courage, intelligence, humanity and determination have been huge parts of that journey and *The Wizard of Oz* is a great starting point in understanding the journey of these actors, and others who soon followed them. The story of the production and legacy of the film is also fascinating, and is explored in the coming chapters.

Prepare to meet some of the most fascinating—and, to put it directly, toughest and hardest-working—people you'll ever meet in the form of the Munchkins of Oz. You should also be prepared for the story of a very demanding film production where people from all walks of life had to work together collectively and learn to respect one another. There are some rather engaging stories of wild times on the set, as well, which have become just as much a part of the mythology of *Oz* as the story itself, and there are plenty of surprises coming up, even for those more or less familiar with *The Wizard of Oz*, the Munchkins and the people who helped craft a film and a genuine cultural legend.

Chapter 2

Gathering the Performers

"The first inkling of *The Wizard of Oz* I got was a letter in the mail with a train ticket that says, 'Come to California to make a movie.'" —Clarence Swensen, actor, from *We're Off to See the Munchkins*.

The *Wizard of Oz* was a major production and, to increase interest in it, the Munchkins were used to promote the film right from the start. MGM needed to have the Munchkins on set by the middle of November 1938. The first call for the actors was launched on November 11.

Twenty-eight of the cast members who played Munchkins were given a ride on a promotional bus. It departed from Times Square and took them across the country, all the way to Culver City, California. The Munchkins were put up in the Culver City Hotel, which allowed them an easy walk to work.

The gathering of the cast, with well over 100 members represented, constitutes the largest gathering of Little People ever assembled for a single project, according to the documentary *We're Off to See the Munchkins*. For the Munchkins, however, getting to the set, and all the promotional activities along the way, were only the beginning. Once they arrived, the real, hard work began.

For some of the Munchkins, however hard the work on the set may have been, there were much greater threats to worry about.

Casting the Munchkins

Many of the actors and actresses that performed as Munchkins were from Europe. Putting this in context, 1938 was the same era when the Nazi party was coming into power and the persecution of various minority groups had already begun. For some of the Munchkins, working on the film allowed them to get away from violent Europe at a time when being different was something more than a liability.

Not all of the Munchkins were from far-flung places, of course. Ruth Duccini, for instance, was from Minnesota. Her acting and performing career started in a small county fair. According to one of her final interviews in The Daily Beast, she and nine of her fellow performers in the troupe she joined at that county fair were all added to the cast of *The Wizard of Oz*.

Some of the actors that played Munchkins were actually children, used to fill out the cast. In the book, Dorothy is greeted by just three Munchkins, but the film, being a huge production, considerably inflated that number, to say the least.

There are some pervasive myths about the Munchkins that remain to this day. For instance, one of those myths holds that a young Elizabeth Taylor played the part of a Munchkin. She did not, however, but the fact that the Munchkins have a group credit rather than individual credits in the film's opening titles makes this sort of rumormongering easy enough to create.

Careers and Backgrounds of the Performers

While this was the 1930s and prejudices against little people were relatively common, some of the actors came from surprising backgrounds. Meinhardt Raabe, for instance, was a flight instructor in the Civil Air Patrol. He was the shortest licensed pilot during the World War II era. He had volunteered to join the army but was immediately turned down due to his size.

While the Munchkin roles may have been the most prominent in many of the actors' careers, they did have other roles and, in some cases, entirely other careers, with *The Wizard of Oz* being the most famous, but certainly not their only, defining accomplishment in life. Here are some of the biographies of the more notable actors and actresses who played Munchkins. Some of the actors and actresses, unfortunately, have faded from history almost completely.

Mickey Carroll

Carroll was born in 1919 and lived a long life, eventually dying in 2009 at the age of 89. He was among the actors who made it to California to receive a star on the Hollywood Walk of Fame. Carroll's career in entertainment was brief, with him leaving the industry to become a maker of cemetery monuments, the Carroll family business. He was a trained dancer, beginning his career when he was 7 years old. He was also a schoolmate of Judy Garland. He played the part of a Munchkin soldier.

Billy Curtis

Billy Curtis was a true performer, having a career that spanned half a century. His roles after *The Wizard of Oz* spanned several genres. He appears in the film *High Plains Drifter*, a western starring Clint Eastwood. He also appears in several science fiction films. He was a member of the Singer's Midgets performing group. Also, he notably appeared in the 1938 western *The Terror of Tiny Town*, which featured a cast made up entirely of little people.

Harry Monty

Harry Monty plays two roles in *The Wizard of Oz* the role of a Munchkin and the role of one of the Wicked Witch's flying monkeys. He had a career that spanned a total of 50 years, and appeared in several television and film roles. He also worked as a stunt person. He was among the little people recruited for *The Wizard of Oz* who had a background as a vaudeville performer.

Olga C. Nardone

Olga C. Nardone lived a very long life, dying at the age of 89 in 2010. She was among the smallest of all the Munchkins, standing at just over 3 feet tall, and played one of the members of the Lullaby League. Like many of the other actors who played Munchkins, she got her start in vaudeville and had extensive training in dance.

Margaret Pellegrini

Margaret Pellegrini was one of the longest-surviving members of the Munchkin cast, living until 2013 and dying at the age of 89. She was among the original cast members who were present to receive their stars on the Hollywood Walk of Fame in 2007. Pellegrini stood at 3' 4" tall and played the part of a sleepyhead.

Meinhardt Raabe

Raabe lived until 2010, dying at the age of 94. He is one of the most noticeable of the Munchkins. He played the coroner who pronounced the Wicked Witch of the East dead. He's also notable in that his real voice appears in *The Wizard of Oz*, where most of the other Munchkin voices were dubbed. Following the film, he joined the Civil Air Patrol and had an MBA. He was married for 50 years.

Raabe appears in a *Newsweek* interview with the original Munchkins, where he takes a bit of a nap during the proceedings. Nonetheless, well into the 2000s, he was still lively, interesting and very proud of the work he previously did on *The Wizard of Oz*.

Ruth Duccini

Ruth (Robinson) Duccini plays the part of a villager in *The Wizard of Oz*. She was among the last surviving members of the Munchkin cast, dying in 2014 at the age of 95. She was among the actresses who showed up for the dedication ceremony on the Hollywood Walk of Fame. Duccini, like many Americans of the time, was part of the war effort during World War II, working on airplanes. She was interviewed by The Daily Beast shortly before she died. She appeared in few roles over the course of her life, but was among the actresses who featured in the 1981 film *Under the Rainbow*.

Duccini was among the last living Munchkins to be interviewed, appearing in the same *Newsweek* interview as did her fellow actors Raabe, Slover, Pellegrini and Maren.

Karl Slover

Slover appears in four different parts in *The Wizard of Oz*. He plays one of the soldiers, a trumpeter, a singer—"Follow the Yellow Brick Road"—and as a sleepyhead. He was a lifelong performer, starting out long before *The Wizard of Oz* as a travelling performer. He was Slovakian by birth. His father had tried various—quack—medical treatments to increase Slover's size, but he went on to become notable for his chops as a performer and a fixture of Oz fandom. He died back in 2011 at the age of 93.

Slover was interviewed by several media outlets over the course of his life and appeared at many different conventions.

Jerry Maren

As of 2014, Jerry Maren is still alive and the last survivor of the original cast of Munchkins. He had a background in performance by the time he appeared in *The Wizard of Oz* and his career in the arts continued long after that film, with Maren appearing in television and film roles well into the 1970s. His career continued in smaller roles until 2010, including roles in *Seinfeld,* horror films and comedies. He is a fixture of Oz fandom as well, though he has recently given up travelling to various events. He was honored by having his handprint and footprint preserved at Grauman's Chinese Theatre in 2013. Born in Boston, he currently resides in California.

Maren recalls his Oz experiences in many interviews, though his life after Oz is just as interesting; and the man became a very accomplished and well-known actor in his own right.

Other Actors and Actresses

With the exception of Jerry Maren, the entire original cast of Munchkins is gone. Many of them, later in life, were featured in parades and other fan events commemorating the film. While the Munchkins, except for Marin, are gone, their legacy very much remains. Actors, however talented they may be, are best remembered for the characters they portrayed and brought to the stage and screen, and the cast that played the Munchkins are no exception to that rule.

The Munchkins, before they became fixtures of film history, worked on a set that was demanding, under conditions that were sometimes exhausting and their exploits became the stuff of legend. While the Oz of the film might be a magical place that existed in the dreams of a young girl, creating it required very real work, and that work is how the film, and the legends surrounding the Munchkins, came to be.

As we progress through the story of the Munchkins on the set and at the hotel, the reader may be waiting for the stories of wild parties and worse that went on. Those are largely exaggerated and were further cemented into the public mind by the film *Under the Rainbow*, in which the Munchkin performers are shown having wild parties and being rowdy almost all of the time.

You'll find the real stories to be far more interesting and the people who played these characters, themselves, to be far more interesting, as well.

Chapter 3

Working in Oz

Filming *The Wizard of Oz*, as one can readily imagine, was no small undertaking. The film is adapted from the book *The Wonderful Wizard of Oz*, of course, and bringing a fantasy epic of such scale to the silver screen required the very best technology and the most advanced filmmaking skills of the time.

Over the course of the film, multiple directors, problems with makeup causing reactions in some of the actors, and the intense heat of the lights required for the Technicolor process would prove to be only some of the challenges that were faced by the cast and crew.

The colossal amount of work that went into the production and the genuine suffering that some of the actors put up with is the stuff of legend as much as is the film itself, and the Munchkins were certainly as much a part of it as the rest of the cast. In fact, some of the hardships of the shoot led to the creation of legends that persist even to this day, though they have been thoroughly debunked.

The Making of an Epic Film

Many of the Munchkins were part of a troupe known as the Singer Midgets. The name derived from the group's manager, Leo Singer. Singing, however, proved to be one of the many challenges that the performers and the production faced.

Because many of the Munchkins hailed from Europe, they naturally had accents. Some of them didn't speak English at all. The Munchkin voices, as anyone who has seen the film can tell, are nearly all dubbed for this sole reason.

When the Munchkins first arrived on set, the actors needed to be sorted out based on their unique skills. Singing and dancing coaches worked with them to figure out which Munchkins were best suited for different roles. Because there were so many actors recruited for these roles, there was a diversity of backgrounds. Some of them had extensive experience in dance and performance, while others had none at all.

Each of the costumes for the Munchkin characters was created individually. While creating over 100 costumes for the Munchkins was certainly a large-scale undertaking, there were over 3,000 created for the entire production.

The makeup director, Jack Dawn, also created individual looks for each of the Munchkins, which were recorded via photographs and subsequently replicated for each day of shooting. The makeup was particularly brutal. The actors would head to the studio at 7 a.m. for makeup and be done by 8 a.m. The makeup included latex skullcaps that were glued into place. According to Lewis Croft, who played a soldier, the process of removing it at night was particularly painful, with the glue that affixed the masks causing sideburns and hair to be pulled out in the process.

The production, however, wasn't all toil and hardship. In fact, for some of the actors, walking onto the set the first day was almost as magical for them as it was for Dorothy to enter Oz in the story.

Scale and Scope

In the documentary *We're Off to See the Munchkins*, actor Meinhardt Raabe described the sets as mind-blowing. Like many of the actors who played the parts of the Munchkins, he hadn't any experience with major productions—certainly nothing on the scale of *The Wizard of Oz*—and was immediately overwhelmed by the size and scale of the sets.

The set is described by Raabe and other actors in that documentary, one of the few places where one can hear the original Munchkins tell their stories of the production, as expansive. Margaret Pellegrini said that she couldn't believe her eyes.

The budget for the film was nearly $3 million in 1938 dollars, eventually going over its budget by a half a million in the end. Adjusted for inflation, that budget would be nearly $50 million today, according to West Egg and the US Inflation Calculator.

Some of the special effects for the film were created using methods that would most certainly not pass muster today. The duck pond, according to Raabe, was a beautiful blue color. Of course, as he points out, blue water is the result of reflected skylight and there was no sky in the studio. The water was dyed blue, thus resulting in live ducklings that also turned blue.

This wasn't the only part of the set and filming methods that betray the times. In the scenes where Dorothy and the rest of her crew fall asleep in the poppy fields, the snow effect was created using asbestos. The makeup used on one of the original actors chosen to play the Tin Man, Buddy Ebsen, caused him to have an allergic reaction and left his lungs coated in aluminum.

Given the budget of the film, there was obviously no room for unprofessionalism. When Judy Garland had a giggling fit after one scene, the director took her aside and harshly slapped her before shooting the next. Two of the flying monkeys wound up in the hospital after the wires that they were using to create the flying effect broke.

For the little people on the set—and everyone else—one of the biggest challenges was working under the intensity of the lights.

Technicolor and Heat

In the documentary *We're Off to See the Munchkins*, several of the actors talk about the incredible heat that was generated by the Technicolor lights. Combine this heat with the costumes and the sheer amount of physical labor involved in acting—remember that these characters do a lot of singing and dancing—and you have a recipe for a very hard day at work.

Raabe relates in the documentary that the lighting for *The Wizard of Oz* was one of the standout features of the set. At the time, according to the actor, the production used more electricity than any film production preceding it. The production made use of two electric generators and the arcs, the industry term for the lights, numbered 100 in total. Those lights were thirty-six inches in diameter and hung precariously from the ceiling, creating the quite convincing illusion that the entire scene was being shot under natural sunlight.

Nels Nelson, who played a villager, talked about the heat. Technicolor was a process that used three separate strips of film in each camera and that required a great deal of lighting for it to be performed correctly. According to Nelson, the heat was brutal and, not long after going under the lights for their performances, the actors would be sweltering in their costumes. As one can imagine, having to wear a non-breathing latex skullcap under those conditions would be brutal on its own, but the actors played their parts in elaborate costumes on top of it, making shoots particularly hot on days when the ambient temperature was already high.

Suffering for Art

Despite the conditions that the Munchkins and everyone else on the set was working under, it doesn't show in the finished project, which is a testament to the abilities of the actors.

While the actors and actresses spent long hours rehearsing their songs and lines, most of what they sang and said was replaced by the voices of professional singers after the film had been shot. The voices that viewers hear on the film are sped up to make them sound higher and, in the end, the only two authentic voices that the audience hears are those of the two Munchkins that see Dorothy off with flowers as she steps into the carriage.

The dancing, the physical acting and the work that went into it are all quite real, however, and producing a Technicolor film was no small, or easy, feat, by any measure.

None of the actors, little people or not, of course, were safe from the technology of the time. The actress who played the Wicked Witch of the West was burned during one shoot due to problems synching the fire in a scene where she had to disappear down a trap door. Pellegrini accidentally fell down a trapdoor herself, as well.

The Legends Surrounding the Little People, According to Those Who Were There

Where most any great film is concerned, there are legends surrounding its production. *The Wizard of Oz* is no exception to this rule, and there are a host of legends that surround it, with some of them being greatly exaggerated, according to the actors that were there on the set and at the hotel after hours to see it all.

One of the most common legends holds that the little people who worked on *The Wizard of Oz,* for the most part, partied like a 1970s rock band in their time off. According to many of the actors interviewed for the aforementioned documentary and in other venues, this is literally the stuff of legend, not grounded in the reality of life on the set. There were, however, some actors who, according to their compatriots, caused more than a few problems for the other little people on the set.

One couple was described by Maren as being particularly problematic. The male half of the couple, Charles Kelly, caused more than one issue, with some of them violent, and the couple was known for their explosive fights.

Kelly once pulled a knife on Pellegrini in her hotel room. According to the actress, she went to open the door and saw Charles standing at the threshold of the door, brandishing a sharp blade. She tried to leave but he insisted that she was going to stay with him, and another one of the little people eventually managed to calm him down.

This sort of behavior did not go without reprimand, of course, and Kelly was "called on the carpet," according to Pellegrini, by Singer the next day and warned that he'd lose his place in the cast if the behavior kept up. Pellegrini, who was very young at the time, and a friend were both moved to a different hotel for their own safety. While this did offer some protection against further assaults by Kelly, it also meant that both actresses had to get up two hours earlier to make it to the set in time for their shoots.

Kelly later showed up on the set sporting two guns, which he was told to leave home by Singer. Singer gave Kelly the choice of leaving the guns off the set or not showing up at all, and Kelly relented at the prospect of losing his job.

One more explosive incident involved Kelly and the friend of Pellegrini who had calmed him down during his first knife-wielding confrontation with the young actress. According to Pellegrini, the cast was eating breakfast one morning when Kelly attacked Jessie, Pellegrini's friend. He grabbed her by the hair and threw her to the ground and several other people had to intervene to pull him off and break up the fight.

Another popular legend surrounds the heavy drinking that the little people got up to, though this is also greatly exaggerated, according to the people who were there. One legend, however, is more or less true and involves one of the little people getting injured and ending up stuck in a toilet, from which he needed to be rescued. While it's sometimes told as a tale that's meant to be amusing, the reality is anything but.

Nelson and Slover related stories about two of the other little people who worked as Munchkins on the production. Their names were Mike and Ike, and they had a reputation for hitting the bottle in their off-time. They'd get rowdy, sometimes getting into fights and keeping other actors awake. One of those actors, Charles Ludwig, was an older fellow who didn't appreciate being kept up.

Mike and Ike, however, got Charles drunk. He wasn't a hard drinker and he had enough to drink with the two men to end up stumbling drunk. He went to the bathroom and fell into the toilet bowl headfirst, desperately crying out for help.

Singer came to his rescue, along with another cast member. Ludwig suffered bruises from the incident and Singer decided to move Ludwig to different accommodations for his own safety.

When Legends Become Unfair

In any large production involving hundreds of people, there are bound to be conflicts and, of course, there are bound to be parties, as well. However, many of the myths and legends surrounding the little people on the set are essentially tales that tell of rampant unprofessionalism and that are uncomfortably similar to the "freak show" mentality that society had toward little people at the time, full of stories of people swinging off of chandeliers, rampant orgies and so forth.

In reality, *The Wizard of Oz* was a demanding production that required a great deal of professionalism from the actors. According to the people that were there, Charles Kelly really stood out as the most troublesome of the bunch, and many of the stories about him are tales that could be told of most heavy drinker with violent tendencies. He was, according to those accounts, abusive toward his wife, abusive toward his fellow actors and prone to brandishing weapons to force his point. One person, however, does not define an entire cast and one must wonder if, were these actors not little people, they would all be lumped together as wild, violent partiers in the legends that surround the production.

In most other regards, the fact that many of the actors and actresses that portrayed the Munchkins comes through in their stories about meeting the biggest stars of the time and of being wowed by the size and scale of the MGM stages and lots.

Some of the big-name stars are remembered particularly fondly by the little people on the set. Mickey Rooney was working on a film at the same time and was, according to Lewis Croft, who played a soldier, very friendly, inviting the actors and actresses to come over and visit him. According to Croft, they did.

Slover mentioned meeting Clark Gable, one of the most significant actors of the time, who invited him and some other actors over to meet him. He described him as a "real nice fellow." Pellegrini also met Gable and other stars and collected autographs and memorabilia from the bigger names she met. Rooney showed up on set quite often, according to Pellegrini, having a crush on Garland and wanting to visit her.

The little people were also given their due respect by the directors— there were five in total—attached to the project. Victor Fleming was remembered particularly fondly by Raabe for being compassionate toward little people and a good person to work with. Fleming was described by the actor as not barking orders and being open-minded to trying different ways of accomplishing shots. Betty Tanner, one of the Munchkin villagers, remembered Mervyn LeRoy as being a nice man, as well. Pellegrini remembers him as carrying her over to first aid when she got a nosebleed during shooting. While this may come off as condescending, given that Pellegrini was a little person, she was young at the time and her memory of it doesn't reveal any signs of being treated like a child so much as being treated with genuine compassion.

Ironically enough, Nelson had particularly fond memories of Margaret Hamilton, who played the notorious Wicked Witch of the West. While her makeup and demeanor was regarded as too frightening for children, Nelson remembers her as the standout as far as friendly members of the cast went. She gave autographed pictures of herself to all of the Munchkin actors and spent enough time with the actors for Nelson to remember her quite fondly.

Judy Garland is, of course, the big star of the film and, despite the fact that she was a teenager, a talented singer, an experienced actress and had the starring role in a major production, she was very easy to work with and didn't treat anyone on stage as her lesser, according to the actors featured in *We're Off to See the Munchkins.*

There's one tale, as related by Pellegrini, that portrays some of Garland's character very well. When Christmas rolled around, the production got Garland her own dressing room. They went so far as to drape it in fabric and wrap it with a red ribbon. Despite receiving such star treatment, Garland remained her very real self. She invited all of the little people to come take a look at the trailer with her. She then gave all of them pictures of herself, each one personalized for the recipient. Pellegrini, who was known for her collection of memorabilia related to the set, still had hers at the time that she was interviewed for the film. Raabe described his autographed photo as his most treasured possession.

While the average-sized people on the set were related as being, particularly among the stars and high-ranking members of the production, respectful toward the little people, for the little people themselves, it was something of a thrill in being on a set with so many other little people.

Building a Community in an Imaginary Land

Maren hadn't seen many other little people, so seeing a set full of them was a memorable experience for him. He describes wondering if the other little people on the set shared his interests and how it was the first time he'd really seen another little person.

Nelson said he'd also lived isolated from other little people and fondly remembered seeing the attractive little women working on the set.

The set itself proved to be a surprising place. When Slover first wandered into the forest set, he wasn't aware that the trees were actually people in costume. He and a friend puzzled over the trees apparently making faces at them until one of the crewmembers let them know that there were actually men inside the trees. The costumes were so convincing, even up close in real life, that Slover was sure that they were actually just trees, or at least very good models of them.

The cast bonded during the holidays that passed during the shoot, spending time together, having their holiday meals at restaurants, watching movies and enjoying other excursions. Maren remembered feeling fortunate to be there at all, working in Hollywood and participating in a major motion picture.

As was mentioned, the studio did pay Toto more than they paid any of the little people. Maren was one of the top earners, pulling in $75 per week, but most of the other actors made far less than this, some pulling in closer to $25 per week.

The actors and actresses who were working for Singer were supposed to receive $100 per week. Singer, however, took $50 out of their pay for himself.

In the documentary, Raabe summed up the arrangement with Singer and the money "What was left after Leo Singer and everybody else took their take, we got fifty bucks a week. Some didn't get that much."

Finishing the Journey

For the little people working on the film, their parts ended on New Year's Eve of 1938. At the time, they didn't have any sense of the impact the film would have, of course, and most of them simply went back to what they were doing before they started shooting on the film. The little people who were performers by trade went back to their work and others simply went home.

The Wizard of Oz, however, really wasn't finished. It would go on to become one of the most significant movies in the history of American film. The film wouldn't premiere for almost a full year after the Munchkins had wrapped their shoot.

Seven decades later, the film remains one of the most beloved of all time. In the coming chapter, the significant impacts that *The Wizard of Oz* had on filmmaking, art, culture and beyond will be explored in detail.

One interesting aspect of this film that will become apparent is how it evolved through the years. While it received very high praise when it was released in theaters and while attendance was good, it really attained its legendary status when television eventually came about, and has endured for generations. The film is more than seven decades old at present, and, if anything, it has only become more respected and beloved during that time.

Chapter 4

After the Release

While fans may obsess a bit over the shooting of *The Wizard of Oz*, a film really doesn't amount to anything until audiences get to see it for themselves. In the case of *The Wizard of Oz*, the film turned out to mean a lot to audiences and, over the years, has maintained a fandom that rivals that of any other cult film or franchise.

The Wizard of Oz, in an odd way, has become as personal a film to its fans as it was to the actors and actresses that made it, including the Munchkins. Before the parades, conventions, magazines and other elements of the fandom could be born, however, the film had to prove itself at the box office, and of course, it did.

The actors and actresses who played the parts of the Munchkins would be a part of the film's success and, in many regards, were among the most memorable and notable characters. They were certainly the favorites of most of the children who saw the film and, in coming decades, would still manage to enchant children and adults alike. Long after the youth of the youngest actors and actresses who portrayed the Munchkins had faded, they would remain significant draws for the public, and many people's favorite characters.

Final Touches

The Wizard of Oz was test-screened before it was finalized and there were some changes made. Some of them were made after test audiences were shown the film. A second rendition of the song "Over the Rainbow" was decidedly deleted from the film. Margaret Hamilton, the Wicked Witch of the West, refused to return for some special effects shots, and a double appears in the film during the scenes where the Wicked Witch flies on a broom that vents smoke.

Hamilton had refused to reshoot the scenes due to the incident related by Pellegrini, when Hamilton was accidentally burned during a special effects sequence that took place in the scenes with the Munchkins. The double who replaced her was also burned during the shoot that Hamilton refused to participate in.

Dance sequences and entire songs were cut from the film to cut down the runtime.

Executive meddling nearly cost the film—and fans—the most memorable song in the entire film. The executives at MGM didn't like the idea of Dorothy singing a song in the barnyard and decided they wanted it removed. Of course, that song stayed in and, in the end, it proved to be a good thing that it did. The song was actually chosen for the number-one spot on a list of the 100 Greatest Songs in American Films by the American Film Institute back in 2004.

Another major plot point in the film is actually the result of executive meddling. The film executives didn't think that audiences would buy that Dorothy travelled to the magical land of Oz. This is why, at the end of the film, the entire experience is revealed to have been just a dream. Of course, while executives may have thought that audiences in 1939 would have been far too sophisticated to have believed that Oz was real, the resulting fandom indicates quite the opposite; people would very much like to believe that it was real after all.

What was real was the impact that the film had, and that started right on the opening night.

Opening Night for a Legend

Opening night for *The Wizard of Oz* came on August 15, 1939 at Grauman's Chinese Theater, or so the story goes. This isn't precisely the case, however.

MGM, with the finished product in hand, were quite convinced that they had a flop on their hands. What's more, they thought they had a *$3 million-dollar flop* on their hands.

In a fashion akin to sticking one's toe in the water to see if it's warm, the studio decided to release the film in a "soft launch." While the Grauman's Chinese Theater premiere is the one most people are familiar with, the film premiered in a much smaller city, Oconomowoc, Wisconsin, a few days before the official premiere in Hollywood. The film does have some strong connections to Wisconsin beyond that. Raabe was a native of the state, as was Herbert Stothart, who wrote the score for the film. The film was also premiered in Kenosha, Wisconsin, and in Cape Cod, Massachusetts, before the major release event.

That first premiere didn't disappoint. Audiences were blown away by the transition from black and white to color and the launch was duly commemorated in Oconomowoc for the 70th anniversary of the film.

What most would consider the real premiere, however, was at Grauman's, and the critics were impressed with what they saw on the screen. The film was described as "delightful," "fantastic" and above all, a success.

Frank Nugent, a film critic of the time, gave the film generally high praise. He said of it that, "A fairybook tale has been told in the fairybook style, with witches, goblins, pixies and other wondrous things drawn in the brightest colors and set cavorting to a merry little score." He did find some of the effects lacking, however, including the Munchkins, saying, "With the best of will and ingenuity, they cannot make a Munchkin or a Flying Monkey that will not still suggest, however vaguely, a Singer's midget in a Jack Dawn masquerade."

While it may have been pointed out in the context of a flaw, the little people who played the Munchkins had been noticed, to be certain. Some of them participated in events to further promote the film, and those interviewed in *We're Off to See the Munchkins* certainly remembered the roles that they played in promoting the film.

Little People Kept on Working at the Premieres

Pellegrini first saw the film in San Francisco. She went with Singer and two other actors. They worked in the lobby before the film, sitting at a table and signing autographs for the filmgoers. She described being very excited at seeing herself on-screen in the film for the first time.

Raabe worked with Oscar Meyer, along with the theater companies, and travelled along with the film as it premiered throughout the Midwest. The promotion involved a six-month stint with the Wienermobile and with Raabe giving the audience some pointers as to what to watch for and hyping the film, all in an Oscar Meyer costume. He described not only the thrill of the premiere, but the fact that many of the small children were scared to the point of tears by the Wicked Witch of the West. During the showings, Raabe remained in the lobby and passed out sample wieners to the audience as they left.

The premiere events did make an impression that lasted long after the film. Maren participated in the premieres in much the same fashion as Raabe—minus the Oscar Meyer costume—and gave the audience some information to get them excited to see the picture itself. Maren had the good sense to hang onto one of the programs from the premiere—he said he should have grabbed more in *We're Off to See the Munchkins*—and he sold it to Christie's Auction House for $3,000.

As for the film's financial success, that did not come easily. The film recorded an initial loss, amounting to more than $1 million in total. That would be more than recouped over time, however. The film was re-released a decade later and earned that money back, plus some more.

The film would become even more profitable as television sets entered the home. It started showing on television in 1956 and it became a tradition to show the film roughly once a year in most markets. This introduced an entirely new generation to *The Wizard of Oz* and, by the time the 1970s rolled around, those children who had watched it on television in the 1950s were watching it with their own children for the second, third, or perhaps fourth time.

This resulted in the fandom that surrounds the film, even today. That fandom and the enduring appeal of the film deserves some consideration.

The Fame—and Sometimes Infamy—of the Film

To put it directly, Dorothy, the Tin Man, the Cowardly Lion, the Scarecrow and the Munchkins are among the most beloved and charming film characters on celluloid. The Wicked Witch of the West and the Flying Monkeys are among the most terrifying for some small children. What does this mean to audiences? A lot, it turns out.

Film critic Roger Ebert, nearly as legendary himself as is the film, considers *The Wizard of Oz* a great film, no small praise from a notoriously tough film critic. In a review written in 1996, he delved deeper into the meaning of the film, noting that its theme of growing out of childhood and entering a strange land is particularly resonant with audiences, which held true even many decades after the film was released.

Dorothy goes off on an adventure that doesn't sugarcoat much of anything. She might be in a magical fantasy land, but that land is full of very real danger. The appearance of the Wicked Witch of the West is still frightening enough, even today, when even most horror films of the 1930s era seem tame at best, and hilarious at worst.

In fact, despite the fact that the film was made decades earlier, the Wicked Witch was *still* considered too scary for children in the 1970s. Margaret Hamilton made a guest appearance on the children's show Sesame Street in 1976. The motivation for the witch to show up was that she dropped her broom while flying over Sesame Street and she needed to recover it. She threatens Big Bird and Oscar the Grouch is quite taken with her. She ends up finding her broom but sticks around on Sesame Street. This episode ends with the witch sticking around, but the episode itself did not. It was only aired once.

In fact, the Wicked Witch was incredibly effective at being terrifying, even outside of Oz where she menaced Dorothy and the Munchkins. Eventually, Mr. Rogers himself had to be called in to calm kids down, having Hamilton on his show where the two explained why kids don't need to be afraid of the Wicked Witch.

Consider most other films of the era of *The Wizard of Oz*, all the way up until the 1970s when the Wicked Witch was apparently still too scary for afternoon television. One would have rare occasion, indeed, to have to explain to a child why rubber monsters in 1950s films aren't scary and would more likely enjoy listening to their children giggle at the silliness. *The Wizard of Oz*, despite its age, is so well made that it can thrill, chill and enchant audiences to this day, all within one story and involving a single cast of characters.

The Munchkins represent the enchanting element of this film. Their friendliness, their sped-up speech and the size of the actors give them a childlike appeal and, as we'll find out when we explore the fandom that surrounds this film, children oftentimes gravitate toward the Munchkin characters most of all. Even the soldiers have the appearance of protectors rather than that of a real threat. The Wicked Witch and her winged primate friends, however, represent the darkest fears that one has when leaving home. They represent powerful and hostile forces and the fear of being overwhelmed and underprepared in the face of danger.

The *Wizard of Oz*, perhaps, has endured because it does embrace the light and the dark of childhood revelry so well. While the Munchkins might be characters of pleasant dreams and, in fact, the sorts of characters that children oftentimes have as their imaginary friends, the Wicked Witch of the West truly lives up to the first word of her appellation and can even give an adult a good chill now and then.

Where the fandom is concerned, the Munchkins ended up being huge draws at conventions, parades and other gatherings. Why could this be? While it will be explored further, one must have a sense that, in their overall meaning and symbolism, the Munchkins are everything that is good about childhood. Innocence, harmlessness and even an entire league dedicated to lullabies. There are few things so comforting and, in those characters, many fans see the real enchantment in this movie, or a good part of it, at least.

For the actors and actresses that portrayed the Munchkins, if they chose to accept and foster it, it meant a lifetime of deserved fame. It meant being a part of a film so huge that it easily overshadowed other, sometimes very impressive, accomplishments and roles, but the shadow cast by *The Wizard of Oz* is certainly not one that is oppressive and is merely a testament to the artistic merit of the film and the quality of the work that the actors and actresses put into it.

The Fame of the Munchkins

The Munchkins ended up being exceptionally popular, and that popularity slowly grew over time. In fact, Wikipedia even has a list of the entire cast of Munchkins, which is far more credit than they received in the actual title cards of the film.

The actors and actresses who played the Munchkins, at least some of them, ended up becoming fixtures at Oz-themed events and, in many cases, were among the biggest draws for the fans.

Pellegrini spent a great deal of time at conventions, having a naturally comfortable way with children and sometimes having to verify to them that she, in fact, really was a Munchkin. Autograph sessions were common and children lined fervently up to meet the people who actually played the Munchkins.

The conventions became some of the best places for members of the original cast to reunite. Many of them ended up attending the conventions for years, including Croft, who said in the documentary *We're Off to See the Munchkins* that he had been going for 10 years at the time the documentary was made and that he and his wife had enjoyed attending, and had met many friends at the conventions.

Betty Tanner, one of the Munchkins who played a villager, had a rather modest take on her popularity when interviewed for the documentary. She said that she didn't feel that she was a celebrity, but that she enjoyed the good feeling she got from the fans' constant adoration.

While some of the actors that played the Munchkins did go on to have very long careers, the roles they played in *The Wizard of Oz* oftentimes remained the ones that fans remember them for the best. Maren said as much, explaining that, when telling fans about other films he has been in, they usually are most impressed with the fact that he was one of the Munchkins. "Forget about everything else, that's it," he said.

Of course, the Munchkins are among the last remaining cast members from *The Wizard of Oz*. Garland and the other big stars of the film are, sadly, mostly gone. There's another aspect to the Munchkins, and to little people, that make them particularly standout celebrities among those who find *The Wizard of Oz* something of an obsession.

The actors who played the Munchkins, of course, retained their physical stature throughout their lives. While the other stars of the film, before most of them were gone, obviously aged and were average-sized adults, the Munchkins were still little people, making it very easy for children to relate to them. While *The Wizard of Oz* may have been filmed more than seven decades ago, the performers who played the Munchkins retained the appeal that they always had, some of them appearing in costume at events and still able to pull off looking like the residents of some magical kingdom from far over the rainbow.

Average-sized actors and actresses likely dream of having a role that creates such an impression on fans. For the Munchkins, their distinctive appearance and the fact that the characters they played were so good and friendly in a world where there were very frightening characters to offset them make them natural favorites of children and adults alike. This film has been seen by several generations now, giving it an opportunity to have fans who are adults who remember the film nostalgically and fans who are children who have just encountered the film for the first time.

The Wizard of Oz and its influence were noticed beyond the film world, however. The film, for some of the actors, provided a springboard to launch very impressive careers. It also marks something of a transition in how little people were portrayed in film and other media. Even today, the term "little people" has replaced the many other cruel and unfair epithets by which little people were sometimes known.

The Wizard of Oz has also spawned a huge fandom, which is explored in the coming chapter, along with an exploration of how the little people who played the Munchkins managed to change perceptions of little people in society at large.

Chapter 5

How the Film Changed Attitudes

There's only one actor left from the entire cast who played the Munchkins in *The Wizard of Oz*. While exploring the changes the film made possible in their lives will be taken up here, the fact that so much time has passed since this film was released gives an opportunity to explore the further-reaching impacts of the film as well.

To put it mildly, little people have, historically speaking, not been treated well or respectfully by society in many different regards. We may live in a far more tolerant age than we did in the 1930s, but some of the leading little people who work in Hollywood still face discrimination, including roles often that play on very unpleasant stereotypes and other hardships.

The Wizard of Oz, however, does serve as something of a milestone in how attitudes have changed over time, and that makes the film significant in regards that go far beyond it just being a great movie.

First, Endure

The Wizard of Oz has a degree of popularity that, first and foremost, gives it the power to change society's perceptions of little people. During the 70th anniversary year of the film, the Belleville Intelligencer out of Canada ran an article about the festivities going on, noting that *The Wizard of Oz* is, arguably, the most-watched film to have ever been made.

With that much reach, the film is in a unique position where influence is concerned. Much smaller films have had huge impacts on society and on social norms, but *The Wizard of Oz* stands out as one that has enormous potential influence, which has been realized in many regards.

In that same article, the first people quoted as authorities on the film are Duccini and Slover, both of whom attended the festivities to celebrate the anniversary. In the article, one doesn't see any sort of reference to little people being made in a condescending fashion and the content focuses largely on the longevity of the film and, as a quote from Jerry Maren makes clear, the true power of the film.

During that year, the film was released in Blu-ray format. It had gone through significant restoration and enhancement efforts, the sort of concentrated and difficult work put into the finest works of art, allowing audiences far too young to have seen it in its original glory to gain a better idea of the experience.

The Wizard of Oz has managed to not only endure, but to be the subject of restoration efforts, an active fandom and, in many different ways, a lot of love on the part of fans. That could be said of many films, but few have been as influential in changing attitudes toward little people and the stigmas often attached to them.

A World of Condescension

There's a difference between hate and ignorance. A hateful person might truly understand the focus of their hatred and, even in the worst cases, hatred can come with a measure of respect. Ignorance, however, has that most obnoxious quality of being completely unaware of itself, and that was certainly the case where the attitudes toward little people were concerned during the 1930s and earlier decades.

As a case in point, among the Munchkin actors was Tiny Schneider. Schneider had several brothers and sisters. Four of his brothers and sisters were little people.

After emigrating from Germany to the U.S. and taking up a life in performance, the family changed their last name to Doll. This came from the insults thrown at the performers by audiences, according to the *Daily Mail*, when the performers would be referred to as "little dolls" by the audiences watching their shows.

One of the children, Daisy, was referred to as the "Midget Mae West" in promotions; not quite herself, just a smaller version of an actual person, the billing seems to imply.

Little people were sometimes cast as freaks, literally. The film *Freaks*, released in 1932, gave a portrayal of little people that, while far less dignified than the one in *The Wizard of Oz*, was likely far more in line with the common attitudes people held toward little people at the time.

In that film, the shock value, in part, is provided by the romantic relationship between a little person and an average-sized woman. The woman is using the little person. The film puts on display some of the cruelty that was visited on people who were different from the norm in any way in those eras, including little people.

In *Freaks*, the little people are part of a travelling show that is not unlike actual shows that existed in this time period and before it. In these shows, people who had no limbs, who had genders that didn't fit within the male/female dichotomy, and who had physical deformities were displayed as if they were curiosities to be marveled at, laughed at or simply taunted.

While the era may have aspects to it that are likely completely foreign to a modern person, people were still people; being singled out, ridiculed and disrespected still desperately hurt, no matter what made someone different from the norm.

Freaks has an ending that exploits the fears that society had—and oftentimes still has—regarding those who are different. The climax of the film involves the sideshow performers taking vengeance on the trapeze artist who's been using the lead little-person character by turning her into one of them. Her punishment, in the end, was to be made different. The level of condescension and bigotry in being made different as a means of punishment is, of course, obscene at best, and heartbreaking at worst.

This is the world little people lived in, to a large extent, during the early 20th century. Little people such as Raabe, as has been noted, were very much isolated from other little people. Take a look at most any film of the era that features a little person and, to varying degrees, you'll get the feel of a freak show in one way or another.

Part of singling someone out is choosing a quality that they have and letting that define them more than they're allowed to define themselves. For actors, actresses and other performers who happened to be small in that era, being a little person was what they were advertised as. The aforementioned Doll family, for instance, had members that performed dance who were noted as being the "smallest dancing couple in the world," according to the *Daily Mail* article referenced above.

One of the most interesting aspects of *The Wizard of Oz* is that it takes little people and puts them in roles where they're actually treated as something special; rather than as something freakish. The Munchkins are part of a magical world and, as such, are seen as magical themselves. They're soldiers and coroners, they have elected officials and, as far as a fairy tale is prone to address such things, they're different in a way that makes them likeable rather than in a way that makes them ripe for the cruel process of othering, as it is sometimes called.

In *The Wizard of Oz*, Dorothy is the freak when she ends up deposited over the rainbow. The Munchkins are legitimate parts of their world and, on top of that, the fact that the Wicked Witch of the East was abusing and dominating them is something that defines her as, would be suggested, wicked.

This is something that, in some sad ways, makes *The Wizard of Oz* even more of a fantasy film. Outside of the studio, in the real world, the little people were still "Singer's Midgets" and Singer still took a hefty chunk of their pay; enough to deserve appellations like "highway robbery" if one is to be honest about it. They were still lumped together as a novelty, even during the opening credits, though it's hard to fault a title card designer for not including everyone's name in the cast listings, considering that there were hundreds that would have had to have been included.

Despite the fact that, as we've seen in previous chapters, many of the little-people actors have mostly fond memories of being part of the production, there are some glaring examples of unfairness and the freak show mentality that existed for years following the completion of the film, and that, to some extent, remain in effect today.

With Friends Like These

Myths, legend and rumors have a way of taking on lives of their own. The Munchkins have been the focus of plenty of each. Even those actors and actresses who were, by the accounts of the little people who worked on the film themselves, nice, played a part in fostering some of the nastiest rumors surrounding the little people.

Going back to that *Daily Mail* article, in the space of one newspaper column, there's enough ignorance to fill a book.

A Judy Garland quote is reproduced in the article entitled "The secret salacious world of the Munchkins." "They were drunks. They got smashed every night and the police used to scoop them up in butterfly nets."

The actual history of what went on at the hotel and on the set have been covered, but there are some glaring inconsistencies between reality and Garland's story that should make it obvious how much of the history of the Munchkin performers has been embellished or outright fabricated by others. It's important to keep in mind that the actors and actresses staying at the hotel were up early, worked a long day and did so for six days each week that they were on the production.

There were drinkers, of course, as has been noted, but the "butterfly net" comment rather invokes the mentality of a genuine freak show. Again, the little people aren't quite like human beings in such a tale. They're not arrested, cuffed and stuffed into the back of a squad car and driven off to the drunk tanks. They're collected with butterfly nets, as if they were wild animals that needed to be kept at a distance, or something less than human beings who would have expected to have been arrested as would any other human being who's had a bit too much drink and gotten a little rowdy.

A quote from Bert Lahr, better known as the Cowardly Lion, is even crueler "Assistants were ordered to watch the midgets who brandished knives and conceived passions for normal-sized members of the cast."

That's not too far from the plot of the movie *Freaks*, of course, and implies that the virtue of average-sized women had to be protected from the knife-wielding, sex-crazed little people that those average-sized women worked with. Of course, like most lies, this one is based somewhat in truth. There were, as was said, incidents that involved little people pulling knives, having domestic disputes and even showing up on set with guns in hand. Of course, all three of those things involved the male member of one couple, who made problems for everyone. Given that the little people are easily singled out, it's suddenly all of them presenting the threat of brandishing a knife and making untoward advances to "normal-sized" people.

It gets worse, and this one article does reproduce three of the most pernicious rumors that have been spread about the little-

people actors that worked on the film. LeRoy, the director, was described as being very nice by several of the actors. In later years, he would be just as unfair in how he remembered the little people, something of a slap in the face considering their rather nostalgic memories of him, on the whole. "They got into sex orgies at the hotel and we had to have police on every floor."

This plays into a popular but painful stereotype of little people. That stereotype casts them as children of a sort. Note the "doll" insults thrown at adult performers working stage and screen shows in the past. Many of the rumors surrounding the cast of little people who worked on *The Wizard of Oz* center on them being somehow out of control or needing constant supervision by peers.

While child actors were used to fill out the ranks of the Munchkins, it's the adult little people who are oftentimes the ones cast as children in these rumors. This contrasts rather starkly with the stories told by the little people themselves, who are, for the most part, fond of remembering their work on the film and the enduring cinematic accomplishments of which they got to be a part of.

There is something of a double-edged sword in all of this. The Doll family is noted in the same article as being somewhat resentful toward the changing attitudes toward little people, which essentially ended their careers as circus performers. The article ponders, in its closing lines, whether better medical treatments for little people will mean that little people will no longer play the parts of the Munchkins in future productions of *The Wizard of Oz* and whether the new generations of performers will be able to conjure up the "rumbustious hijinks" of the original performing Munchkins.

If the high-jinks that the article laments may be things of the past include getting up early for work, enduring very difficult—and sometimes dangerous—shoots and creating great art in the process, there are plenty of little people who work as actors who should be able to "conjure up" such high-jinks today.

None of the Munchkins Hanged Themselves

One of the rumors that has persisted, probably due to its inherently morbid nature, does invoke the conditions under which the actors and actresses who played the Munchkins toiled. While the rumor is described in detail below, it's easy enough to answer this rumor without delving too deep into it for those who simply want to know No Munchkins killed themselves during the performance; you cannot see a hanging little person actor in the background during a scene in *The Wizard of Oz*.

This is how the story goes, and it's been circulating for a very long time.

One of the actors who played a Munchkin was in love with one of the female little people who was also in the film. She didn't love him back and, despondent over that, he simply hanged himself. In the scene where Dorothy and the Scarecrow have discovered the Tin Man and head off down the Yellow Brick Road, if one looks in the background of the scene, one can see the deceased little person in the background, still suspended where he hanged himself.

This has been dispelled by Snopes and others and, on the face of it, goes beyond being ridiculous and it steps firmly into the territory of being downright stupid.

The figure that one sees in this scene—people weren't hallucinating this—was originally thought to be just some stagehand or another who had failed to get out of the shot before the cameras started rolling. This wouldn't be hard to believe, given that there are some spots here and there where, despite the fantastic amount of work that went into the film, one can see some obvious flaws. Of course, the stories of injuries and accidents on the set are real, in some instances, making this one seem plausible enough.

It's not far from the truth. According to the research into the matter that Snopes did, the background figure is actually a large bird. There were many animals brought onto the set to give the film a more realistic feel. Recall Raabe's story about the dyed-blue ducks. One of those animals had apparently wandered into the background of the set, where it can be seen roaming around a bit.

People obsessed over this and, soon enough, one of the most persistent rumors surrounding the film was invented. Snopes notes that this rumor became particularly popular during the 50th anniversary celebration of the film and that it also stuck around long after.

As their research notes, this is a rather hard thing to believe if one uses even the simplest logic. It would require the entire crew—which was huge—not noticing that there was a dead man hanging from a tree. It also flies in the face of what the Munchkin players have already revealed about the production. It was a busy affair, with electricians and lighting techs constantly on the lookout for too-intensely focused lighting. The detail on the sets and in the costumes was such that some of the actors didn't realize that the apple trees even had people in them. Thus, it was hardly a production where things go unnoticed!

Like most of the rumors surrounding the Munchkins, this one is pure nonsense. It plays nicely into the stereotype of little people being out of control and, essentially, children who need to be supervised. It also plays nicely into the preferences of those who thrive on conspiracies. In that light, the conspiracy would have involved hiding the suicide—visible on film, no less—of a little-person actor who was a member of a troupe for which all members have been accounted for over and over again by historical researchers far and wide.

It's ridiculous, and it never happened. In fact, as we've seen, most of the actors and actresses who played Munchkins were glad to be on the set and the ones who were surly, drunk and violent were very much the exceptions, and certainly not the rule.

There is no deceased Munchkin visible in any frame of *The Wizard of Oz*, no matter how morbidly attractive some may find that rumor and no matter how many Internet pages it has been reproduced on. It just didn't happen.

Getting to the Positive

In a 1997 *Lodi News-Sentinel* article, August Clarence, who was 79 at the time, said that *The Wizard of Oz* helped to change the image of little people, and there is some significant truth to that.

While there are plenty of rumors, some of them rather nasty, that have popped up over the years surrounding this film, there are also plenty of good realities that came about because of it, particularly for little people and, even more so, for little people who work in arts and entertainment.

Times have changed—considerably—since the days when *The Wizard of Oz* was filmed. Like the four protagonists in the film, however, little people have travelled a long road to get from there to here. It would be naïve to say that one film is responsible for the changes in society that have since given little people acceptance as people, rather than as curiosities, but *The Wizard of Oz* did make its fair contribution. It made a very big difference in the lives of many of the little people who worked in the film, and some of those differences were quite personal, invoking a lot of work and leading to very impressive careers.

Little People as Actors After Oz

The Wonderful Wizard of Oz was only one of a series of books that L. Frank Baum authored that took place in the magical land. Of course, this wasn't lost on Hollywood and Oz continues to be a frequent destination of film writers, with the most recent movie being *Oz the Great and Powerful*, directed by Sam Raimi and starring James Franco.

That film also employed little people to play the parts of Munchkins. Like the original actors, many of the Munchkins who appear in this newest film come from backgrounds that are very conventional. Like those original actors, they also hoped that their work on this film would help little people to get more work and recognition for what they can do. Interestingly, two of the actors that appeared in that newest Oz-themed movie got noticed because of their previous work in an Oz-themed commercial.

Two of the actors, Robert and Mary Hall, appeared in an ad for AAA 30 years before the new Oz film was made, according to MLive. The commercial featured a pitch for homeowners insurance where a house crashes to the ground and where a salesperson shows up and assures the owners that they have adequate coverage.

It's light and funny, of course, as it's meant to be, but it does show how a movie made in 1939 has become so easily recognizable that some of its hallmark scenes can be instantly recognized by audiences—and how much the Munchkins are a part of that instant recognition.

After *The Wizard of Oz* wrapped, some of the little people who were cast members found themselves with acting careers that they never expected to have, and going on to become very well-established Hollywood figures after their first break at the beginning of the Yellow Brick Road.

Those That Went on to Hollywood Careers

There are really few roles available for little people at any given time in Hollywood. While there are more little people working in Hollywood playing characters who are defined by their personalities and abilities as much as they are by their size—*Game of Thrones* being a prime example of this, with a little person being one of the smartest and most capable characters on the show—little people oftentimes have to branch out a bit in order to have a full-fledged career in Hollywood. *The Wizard of Oz* helped some of them to do just that.

In *The Independent,* Jerry Maren revealed how his work on *The Wizard of Oz* helped him to secure a firm foothold in Hollywood.

Maren was approached as soon as the film wrapped and told that, not only did the studio want him for another role—in a film called *Tiny Troubles*—but that they wanted him to be the star of the film. This was the era of the studio system and films were written and produced at a very fast pace. Maren, essentially, went right to working on the new film and, after that one was finished, he was ready to head back home. Heading home was not on the cards for him.

Maren went on to work on a Marx Brothers film, *At the Circus.*

After that, Maren just kept on working. He still works in Hollywood today and, as has been noted, is the last of the original Munchkins still alive. He's won awards for films that are certainly off the beaten path for someone so associated with fantasy film, receiving a 2011 Action Film award from the International Film Festival, USA, for his work in *Dahmer vs. Gacy.* In addition to this, he has 40 acting credits in total on IMDb, along with more than 20 television credits, 2 stunt credits and much more. While *The Wizard of Oz* may have kicked off Maren's career, he's attended to it well since, and that's a certainty.

Margaret Pellegrini went on to become a fixture of Oz fandom and was the second-to-last Munchkin alive until 2014. Her filmography is much shorter than Maren's, but she did work—uncredited—in *Johnny Got His Gun,* a World War I film from 1971 that tells the story of a man who loses his arms, legs, voice, hearing and sight during an intense battle.

Pellegrini was also featured in several documentaries about *The Wizard of Oz* and continued to give interviews to newspapers and other media outlets about her experiences late into her life.

Ruth Duccini had two film credits, the second being *Under the Rainbow,* and appeared in documentaries where she shared her memories. She also appeared on *The Daily Show with Jon Stewart.*

As was said, roles for little people in Hollywood are notoriously few and far between, and some of the Munchkin players quickly faded into obscurity after appearing in *The Wizard of Oz*. Many of them, however, went on to become very popular at the many Oz-themed events held since the movie debuted. Fans generally prized any memories that they could share and, even so long after the film was released, many of them found themselves in consistently high demand.

What's Changed Since the Filming

While little people are still not seen nearly as much as average-sized people in films, the roles they play as entertainers and celebrities have certainly expanded. In fact, today, little people are found not only in acting roles, but in even more demanding roles in the entertainment world.

Case in point Jason Acuna is better known as "Wee-Man." He's a fixture on the show *Jackass* and he's an accomplished skateboarder and exceptionally daring stunt person. He actually uses his size to pull off stunts that the average-sized people likely couldn't, and has a good time surprising the unsuspecting while doing so.

Bushwick Bill is a rapper with the controversial group Geto Boys. He's got a reputation as hard as that of any other rapper in his genre, and his height makes him memorable rather than a novelty.

Peter Dinklage is an American actor whose reputation is something beyond stellar. He plays the character Tyrion Lannister on the HBO series *Game of Thrones*. While his resume is extensive, the Tyrion Lannister character is a particularly interesting one for him to portray. A little person, he faces ceaseless bigotry from the people around him, but uses his superior intellect to utterly dominate and defeat many of his rivals. It's an uncommon role for a little person to get, where his size both is and is not a major part of who he is. Ironically, his first major role was in the film *Living in Oblivion*, where he played an actor trying to get beyond roles that offered him nothing but stereotypical characters.

Not all little people find the roles of Munchkins—and related small characters, such as elves—to be particularly flattering, however.

In 1999, a *Baltimore Sun* article addressed this issue head-on. The article centered on an audition for a promotional gig for an upcoming stage play of *The Wizard of Oz*. Not one little person showed up to audition for the Munchkin roles; as they were all children.

Marty Kebbla, a little person who was directing the auditions, was sympathetic to the fact that many little people would like to see fewer of their number playing these roles. Some little people find them degrading. The article describes a six-foot-tall man auditioning for one of the roles, making mocking imitations of the Munchkins' movements and singing in a falsetto while he does it. Kebbla referred him to the unemployment line, and took offense at the childish portrayal.

It's easy to see why. An uncomfortably written *LA Times* article from 2008 covers how two of the child actors who played the parts of Munchkins were not invited to the ceremony where the star on the Walk of Fame was installed for the Munchkins. The author of the article, Stephen Cox, makes a remark that there was nothing about "midgets only" at the ceremony, using a term that little people have tried very hard to get people to stop using, as it carries with it years of objectification and unprecedented prejudice.

There's still a mixed bag to be dealt with where the legacy of the Munchkins and the acceptance of little people is concerned. Some people may find the original Munchkins to be an example of a great, breakthrough role for little people, while others find that it reflects the objectification of little people that was the norm at the time.

Whatever one's feelings on the matter, it's indisputable that *The Wizard of Oz* garnered for itself an incredibly large and loyal fan base. That fan base has, over the years, held many different events and gatherings and the Munchkins are typically significant features of those events, as was pointed out in the actors' own unique recollections.

The next chapter takes a look at the phenomenon of Oz fandom and the role of the Munchkins within that subculture. *The Wizard of Oz* might be over seven decades old, but it still enchants people of all ages.

Part II Oz, Its Importance and Its Legacy

The Wizard of Oz ended up becoming one of the best-known and most beloved films of all time. It also created an entirely new fairytale mythology. As we've seen, the Munchkins were a huge part of that and they continued to figure prominently into many a reimagining of Baum's world long after the 1939 film was released.

This next section tells the story of the fandom, memorabilia, art and other elements associated with the Oz universe. To begin with, however, we'll take a look at some of the many films that have been released that took place in Baum's world. Some of them are remakes of *The Wizard of Oz* in one way or another. Others take place in the same world, but provide new material for audiences to digest, much to their delight, in most cases. Still, others weren't so well received but, given that they are a part of the legacy, they still have a place here.

The actors and actresses who played the Munchkins couldn't have had any idea what they were participating in when they showed up for those first days on the set. They ended up being part of a legend, and entirely new mythology and the collective stories, symbols and memories that constitute this unique and very American fairytale land.

Chapter 6

The Film, Later Adaptations, and Related Movies

The *Wizard of Oz* only grew more influential over the years following its release. A great deal of that influence was because of the regular television showings of the films, during which entirely new generations of fans were instantly created. Those fans, familiar with the mythology of Oz, were a natural market for further explorations of the land and its denizens.

L. Frank Baum left behind many books that further developed the fantasy land, offering numerous different opportunities for filmmakers and later writers to expand it beyond Baum's visions. What started as a tale that was about a girl and her dog and their adventure in Oz, soon became a legendary setting for wild imaginings and, over the decades, there have been several films that were released that allowed the world further exploration into Oz.

There are also films that concerned the Munchkins themselves to varying degrees; some good, some not so good. What follows are some of the films that derived from *The Wizard of Oz* and other Baum originated ideas.

It's always best to start from the beginning, as Dorothy found, so we'll start from the silent era, with the 1925 production of *The Wizard of Oz*, which bears little resemblance to the 1935 version, and certainly hardly any resemblance to the book.

The Wizard of Oz (1925)

Director

Larry Semon

Starring

Oliver Hardy

Dorothy Dwan

Larry Semon

Bryant Washburn

The 1925 version of *The Wizard of Oz* bears almost no resemblance to the book on which it is ostensibly based. It claims L. Frank Baum Jr. in its writing credits, but it's not widely agreed that he had much influence on the film beyond lending his name to it and then promoting it.

The film gives us a much different story and, if you're looking for the Yellow Brick Road and other elements that are more or less shared between most other versions, you're not going to find them here.

The Plot

This film opens up with a toymaker, who opens up a book to reveal the credits of the film. From the start, it's much different than fans of Oz will expect. The story holds that Dorothy is actually a long-lost princess of Oz and that the land is currently ruled by Prime Minister Kruel and Lady Vishuss, his able aide, as the film holds. Ambassador Wikked rounds out the appropriately-named villains.

The people of Oz aren't happy with their ruler, but they have an advocate in Prince Kynd. The people want their queen to return to them, something that Prime Minister Kruel, of course, wants to prevent from happening, so he sends Wikked to make sure that it doesn't.

Dorothy is about to turn 18 in this film. She lives with Aunt Em and Uncle Henry in this film, but Uncle Henry is not a kind and loving man. On the contrary, he's actually horrible. Their farmhands are also not particularly well treated and, in fact, they're certainly not de facto members of the family as they are in the 1939 film.

In the 1939 film, there's a sort of affection between Dorothy and Hunk/The Scarecrow. In this film, two of the farmhands have obvious crushes on her. Oliver Hardy and Larry Semon play the farmhands who develop feelings for Dorothy.

Dorothy turns 18, but there's a family secret involved. Dorothy is not really related to Aunt Em or Uncle Henry. She was abandoned on their doorstep as a young baby. With the child was an envelope that had instructions that she was to open it when she was 18 years of age.

The note tells that Dorothy is actually Princess Dorothea of Oz. When she reads the decree in the envelope, her position will be secured and, to prevent that from happening, Wikked shows up.

The film quickly turns dark, with Wikked threatening to kill Dorothy if Uncle Henry doesn't give him the envelope. Hardy tries to curry Wikked's favor—and Dorothy's love, as promised by the villain— by giving Wikked the note he seeks. Fortunately, he's prevented from doing so by Semon.

The tornado is present in this story, and just as in the 1939 version, it whisks them off to Oz. There's no Wicked Witch this time, however. Dorothy reads the letter. To avoid being punished for their roles in helping Dorothy to get and read the letter, Kruel accuses them of kidnapping Dorothy and wants the Wizard of Oz to turn them both into monkeys. He doesn't, but they end up in jail nonetheless. Hardy becomes the Tin Man—simply a disguise in this film—and Semon becomes the Scarecrow. Hardy eventually betrays his friends and gets them sent to jail.

Hardy turns out to be rather villainous himself and Dorothy and Prince Kynd have token positions in the government. Henry and Hardy, neither of whom deserve it, come into power in Oz under the Prime Minister.

Prime Minister Kruel decides that he needs to marry Dorothy so that he remains in power. The Wizard of Oz appears in the story and gets the farmhands out of jail and Dorothy is told that Kruel is merely using her to further his plans.

Kruel gets busted for being the one that sent Dorothy to Kansas. Semon is in love with Dorothy, but she's already fallen for Prince Kynd and instead decides to marry him. Semon is chased by Hardy and Wikked and, apparently, gets killed in the process. The film ends with Dorothy walking up and, after she falls back asleep, the toymaker from the beginning of the film reads that Dorothy and the Prince lived happily ever after.

Not Related

While the 1939 *Wizard of Oz* took some liberties with Baum's source material, this film has almost nothing to do with it at all. It's essentially a different story with the same characters and some of the same places. There are no inklings of the little girl Dorothy that audiences came to love as portrayed by Judy Garland. The Tin Woodsman, Cowardly Lion and Scarecrow are all here, however, in very different renditions.
The farmhands, rather than being supportive and loving toward Dorothy, spend their time trying to impress her and engaging in slapstick hijinks on the farm. Uncle Henry is downright mean.

The entire motive with the letter, Dorothy actually being Princess Dorothea and the rest of it are likely to be entirely new concepts to fans of Oz, as are the comically named villains.

The Scarecrow in this film –Semon—is really more important of a character than is Dorothy and, really, is also more likeable. Dorothy is something of a vixen in this film. The Tin Man is an outright villain, which is a far cry from the character in the book and most certainly from the lovable character that appears in the 1939 film, who is, according to Dorothy, among the best friends that anyone could have. Certainly, Hardy does not meet that definition and, even more so, he's not even a Tin Man, just a villain who has disguised himself cleverly.

Is it Worth Watching?

If you're looking to learn more about Baum's universe, you'll do better to read the novels or to watch the other adaptations of the material listed in this section. This film has little to do with them, but that doesn't mean that it's not worth watching. In fact, it is most certainly worth watching.

Oliver Hardy became famous for his physical abilities as a comedian and, in some scenes, those abilities are very much on display here. This is a silent film, so the actors have to speak with their expressions and their movements and it's interesting to see how they manage to pull it off.

This is not a bad film at all. If you happen to pick up any of the official re-releases of *The Wizard of Oz* from 1939, this film will be included, as well, as it's now in the public domain and it's free for anyone to distribute. You can also watch it online at YouTube and at other sites.

Interestingly, though this film is in black and white, it does make use of different film tints to denote different places and varying emotions. For instance, most of the scenes at the farm are sepia toned, but it switches over to a bluish tint during the storm and when the characters end up in Oz, some of the scenes have a purplish-red tint to them that gives them a sense of place. It's not Technicolor, of course, but it does add something unique to the mix.

Don't expect the makeup and costumes to be on the same level as they were in *The Wizard of Oz*. Remember that *The Wizard of Oz* was, in every regard, a production that pulled out all the stops and redefined movie making in many ways. The 1925 vision of *The Wizard of Oz* is a silent film that is sometimes interesting, sometimes not so much that that is worth seeing for anyone who has an interest in film history and, in particular, who wants to see a very different imagining of Frank Baum's Oz universe.

The 1925 has over-the-top acting, melodramatic villains and some genuinely silly names for them, to boot. Keep in mind, however, that you're not going to be as enamored with Dorothy as you will be in the 1939 version, there aren't any Munchkins to be found and the scale is much smaller and as a result; less impressive.

The Wizard of Oz (1939)

Director

Mervyn LeRoy

Starring

Judy Garland

Frank Morgan

Ray Bolger

Bert Lahr

Billie Burke

Margaret Hamilton

Saying that *The Wizard of Oz* is a great film is, oddly enough, probably understating it. This film has captured the imaginations of several generations now. In a world where spectacular CGI effects are seen even on low-budget television shows, this film's special effects still enchant viewers.

The plot of the film is important, of course, but as is the case with any fairy tale, the plot isn't the most important thing in this film, just one of many important elements.

We're going to look at this film in ways that you might not have thought of before. There is another chapter later on that gives some of the more interesting interpretations of this film, including interpretations that derive by comparing the original book, *The Wonderful Wizard of Oz* with the 1939 film version.

To begin with, however, *The Wizard of Oz* offers plenty of material to dig through. Like the Land of Oz itself, the movie is mysterious, sometimes delightful and fun and sometimes it is downright frightening. This is a children's tale on the level of a Grimm fairy tale. It has the kind of power in its narrative and execution that will likely guarantee that it will be regarded as important for just as long as those legendary fairy tales from long ago.

As we go through this, keep in mind that this film is close to 100 years old now, and it still holds a tremendous amount of power. This is what happens when talent, vision and technology all come together at once. Something magical happens, and not just in the narrative of the film. There is real magic in how the film itself plays out, and we'll explore that in greater detail.

The Plot More than a Summary

The plot of the *Wizard of Oz*, if we strip it down to its barebones, is, in part, so powerful because it is so classic. In essence, this is a quest film. Dorothy finds herself in a strange land and, to reach her ultimate goal, she has to complete a quest. In fact, she has to complete two quests. First, she has to get to the Emerald City. Second, she has to get the Wicked Witch of the West's broom.

We start out with a young girl on a farm. She's surrounded by regular people, both good and not so good. She has people around her who clearly care about her, but they're hardworking farm people and it's clear that there's really not much destined in this life for a little girl. The sepia tone in the Kansas sequences is gorgeous, but devoid of color.

Dorothy has one woman who is a sort of nemesis already, Miss Gulch, who is about as appealing as the name implies. She's a nasty old woman and she wants to have Dorothy's dog, Toto, killed for biting her on the leg.

Toto manages to get away from Miss Gulch and Dorothy, loving her dog as she does, decides to take off with him. They make it to a fortuneteller and he sends her back home with a bit of trickery.

The sequence in this film where Dorothy's house gets caught up in the twister is one of the most dramatic and, particularly for the time, the effects are certainly convincing enough. We also get a bit of foreshadowing that what's going on is in Dorothy's head. The scene where Miss Gulch turns from a bicycle-riding nuisance into the

Wicked Witch of the West is particularly telling. Keeping in mind that the studio executives thought that audiences would be too sophisticated to swallow the idea that a little girl goes off to a fantasy land makes this even more significant. This is the beginning of Dorothy's vivid hallucination.

The Munchkins

Because the Munchkins and the little people who played them are really the focus of this book, it's worthwhile to give them some extra attention in terms of the plot. When Dorothy arrives, the village is very quiet, the Munchkins having simultaneously endured having a dingy farmhouse drop on their village and the death of the oppressive Wicked Witch of the East.

Of course, this is where Glinda, the Good Witch of the North shows up. She's the antithesis of the Wicked Witch of the West that we're about to meet. She's kind, speaks in a voice befitting a Kindergarten teacher and believes Dorothy to be a witch at first. Once Dorothy explains what's going on, Glinda takes on a sort of quest-giver role because as mentioned above, in many regards, *The Wizard of Oz* is, in fact, a quest film.

The Munchkins—and the actors who played them—were obviously cast for their proportions. They appear very childlike here. The village is very colorful; and a huge flower sits at its center. This, again, is a bit different than how Munchkinland was envisioned in Baum's books. If it were truer to the book, it would have been far more monochromatic, but the effect works marvelously in the Technicolor.

For those with a more technical mindset, it's impossible not to see the tremendous about of direction that must have gone into these scenes. Soldiers and villagers, the Lullaby League, the Lollipop Guild and the rest of the population of Munchkinland come out, complete with plenty of singing and dancing.

In these first scenes in Oz, it's also possible to see, for the first time in the film, the incredible amount of light that was used on the set. When the actors and actresses who played the Munchkins talked about the lighting on *The Wizard of Oz*, they clearly were not exaggerating. The brilliance of the colors is brought out by the bright light that floods the entire scenes. For those who are most interested in the technical aspects of this film, it's truly remarkable how they managed to flood a set with so much light and still keep the rich shadows that give the scene its true depth.

The Munchkins are kind, friendly and welcoming. They seem to start singing at the drop of a hat. One might imagine that it's because they're happy to finally be done with the Wicked Witch of the East or simply because they're magical creatures and that's just the way that they communicate with one another. It makes them memorable, to say the least.

The director made the most of the set, filling it with villagers and finally having Dorothy literally start out her journey at the beginning, as Glinda suggests, by going to the central spiral where the Yellow Brick Road ends in Munchkinland and start walking outward, her first steps toward Oz.

Glinda also explains the terms of the deal, essentially, as far as getting to Oz is concerned. She has to hang onto the Ruby Slippers or she'll be at the mercy of The Wicked Witch of the West. Glinda also gets a pretty good line in on the Wicked Witch of the West, telling her to be gone before "somebody drops a house on you, too."

By some accounts, this is the transition where Dorothy starts journeying from childhood into adulthood or, if one takes the larger metaphor look, moving from the traditional life of the farm and farm workers—the Munchkins—to the mysterious city where the Wizard of Oz lives.

The Munchkins send her off with "Follow the Yellow the Brick Road", of course, and she skips her way out of their village with Toto off onto the Yellow Brick Road.

The Yellow Brick Road Trip

Dorothy meets the Scarecrow first, runs into the apple orchard where the trees object to having their apples picked and runs into the Tin Man, who's frozen in place because he has not been oiled.

It's worth noting how innocent Dorothy is in this film. She first runs into a talking Scarecrow and, rather than being petrified, frees him and gets a friend. The Tin Man, when she meets him, is standing with is axe raised in the air and asks to be oiled. She does, trusting that, in a world where she already knows a witch is out to get her, and he'll be an ally, too.

The three decide to go off to see the Wizard together, but the Wicked Witch of the West soon shows up and starts threatening them again. While the visage of the Wicked Witch of the West is pretty intense for the young audience that usually watches this film, she mostly just threatens Dorothy in particular. She doesn't actually do much to stop the trio from making their way out of the forest and to the Emerald City.

There are callbacks to the fact that Dorothy is hallucinating this entire scenario throughout the film but one of the most noticeable is when she mentions that she feels like she's known the Tin Man and Scarecrow for her entire life, which, of course, she has.

Rather like the Wicked Witch of the West, the Cowardly Lion is essentially all mouth when the trio first meets him, ending up being admonished and driven to tears by a little girl. He ends up joining them, of course, thus rounding out the quartet of friends and heading off down the road.

Among the most impressive sets on this film is the poppy field. She can see the Emerald City off in the distance but, unfortunately, they head right off through the poppies, exposing Dorothy to the Wicked Witch of the West's sleeping spell, the Coward Lion soon falls asleep, as well.

Interestingly, the Tin Man is genuinely upset by what's going on, showing that he does have a heart. The Scarecrow thinks to yell for help, getting Glinda's attention, showing that he does have a brain.

In a bit of a frightening twist, the snow that falls all over the poppies is actually asbestos.

When they finally make it to the Emerald City, Dorothy gets to see the full glory of the urban world. A friendly cabby offers to take the group to clean up and get comfortable in a carriage pulled by the famous Horse of a Different Color.

The group gets to experience the luxuries of city life, with Tin Man getting buffed, the Scarecrow getting stuffed and the Cowardly Lion getting his hair trimmed. Dorothy gets cleaned up, but it's not long until the Wicked Witch shows up and advises Dorothy to Surrender by way of a smoking broom she uses for skywriting.

The Cowardly Lion gets a number that foreshadows what Dorothy's about to need; which is a lot of courage. Dorothy also gets a moment to confront failure and takes some responsibility for abandoning her family. The guard is moved and decides to get the Wizard for Dorothy after she's rejected at first.

The Wizard proves as intimidating as promised, with plenty of pyrotechnics, smoke and appearing as a huge, deformed green head. The Cowardly Lion ends up diving through a window in order to get away.

Next comes the Haunted Forest, complete with a grammatically incorrect sign leading to the "Witches Castle". The group is armed this time, however, the Tin Man with a pipe wrench, the Scarecrow with a butterfly net and a revolver and the Cowardly Lion with a hammer. Still, it doesn't do them much good. The Flying Monkeys are dispatched to devastating effect, bringing Dorothy back to the castle alive at the Wicked Witch's behest.

This is probably one of the most frightening sequences in the film and it is likely to have caused more than its share of frightening dreams. In fact, it's one that TV Tropes puts in the category of "High Octane Nightmare Fuel".

The gang ends up at the Witch's Castle, of course, and eventually Dorothy manages to melt the Witch with a bucket of water. The Scarecrows shows some brains when he realizes that he can drop a chandelier on the Witch's guards simply by loosening a rope.

After they all make it back to the Emerald City, Dorothy finds out from Glinda that she had the power to go home all along. She says goodbye to her friends and immediately wakes up in Kansas, apparently having taken a hard blow to the head during the tornado. She's convinced that she was in a real place but, surrounded by her friends and family, she realizes that there's no place like home after all, saying as much in one of the film's iconic lines and bringing the film to a close.

What Made this Film Endure

The Wizard of Oz has been around for so long that it's easy to see it as a rather conventional fairytale. This is accurate, but not because of it being derivative. It actually redefined fairytales while still playing into one of their most important elements.

Everyone in this story is looking for something that they already have. They're all looking for whatever they believe will make them a complete person in some far off place, but they all have that within them already. Dorothy has this happen to her several times. She thinks the Wizard can get her home, but finds that he's just a charlatan. She then finds that, without any magic at all, he can get her home, but misses her chance when Toto takes off after a cat.

Of course, her travel companions already have exactly what they were after, as well. When Dorothy finally confronts Miss Gulch in her guise as the Witch, she finds that she can be taken out by the most mundane of things. For all her bluster and threatening, she's just a weak old crone who really isn't much of a threat once Dorothy tosses a bucket of water at her. Dorothy does it to protect her friend, the reason that she was fleeing in the first place, to protect Toto.

The film, for an adult, likely seems nostalgic and entertaining and brings back childhood memories. Interestingly, it still stands on its own alongside the newer offerings that are available for children. Even the sets, with their obviously—but beautifully—painted backgrounds are enough to keep children interested, in a world where CGI can make much more convincing landscapes than we're seeing here.

For the Film Buffs

People who truly love film tend to see a lot of importance in the ones that they adore, and this one offers that in many regards.

The special effects might be lacking here and there, but that's simply because of the time in which the film was made. When the era is taken into account, they're really quite spectacular. Glinda's bubble hits a few bumps here and there. The scenes where the Wicked Witch is flying by sometimes obviously involves a puppet, as do the flying monkeys.

There's enough here, however, that suspending disbelief is actually fun for those involved in watching this film. In fact, "involved" is precisely the right term here. This moving is involving.

The Wizard of Oz has never worn out. It has never become stale or old and it's still a regular feature on today's television. With it having moved onto cable, it's shown more than ever, introducing Dorothy's story to an entirely new generation of fans.

Not everyone will end up being an Oz fanatic because of this film. Some might even mind the musical numbers a bit distracting, as musicals went out of vogue, for the most part, long ago. Nonetheless, this film consistently gains new fans, keeps old fans tuning in, and is every bit on the level of other fare that was aired yearly on network television, including Christmas and Halloween specials which everyone remembers.

The Wizard of Oz was a marvelous technical achievement for the time. It was an enormously expensive film and the shoot pushed actors to their physical limits. There were injuries and even hospitalizations.

The film, however, from the Munchkins to the farmhands to Auntie Em is about the remarkable nature of ordinary people and how, when we really want something, sometimes the best place to look for it is within ourselves and in those around us.

The Wiz (1978)

Director

Sidney Lumet

Starring

Diana Ross

Michael Jackson

Nipsey Russel

Ted Ross

Lena Horne

Richard Pryor

The Wiz is a cinematic adaptation of a stage play of the same name. It features an African-American cast and significantly updated, and far more urban, surroundings all around. The soundtrack is also much different from the original, with a funky feel and an edgy modern twist. Michael Jackson is featured in this film.

Different Story, Same Themes

Our heroine in this film doesn't live on a farm, but instead she lives in the city. She's transported to Oz by a magical snowstorm instead of a tornado. The sets are very urban in this film.

When Dorothy Gale meets the Munchkins, they don't live in a small village. In fact, they've been turned into graffiti, a fate from which Dorothy saves them.

The rest of the story unfolds in essentially the same fashion as it does in the 1939 production. Dorothy has to make her way to the Emerald City to find her way home. The Yellow Brick Road is literally littered with yellow bricks rather than being a solid road made out of gold bricks when Dorothy and the Scarecrow first find it, singing a rendition of "Ease on Down the Road" as they do.

Dorothy is sent on the same quest by the Wizard and gets home in essentially the same fashion as she does in the first film, but the home, unlike any other place in this film, is New York City.

The musical changes in this film are really the standout features. The scenery isn't as fantasy like as it was in the original, which also gives it a new feel that fits with the era in which it was released. There are some interesting elements to this story that really make it something to see if you're one of the world's many Oz fans.

More than a Small Update

At first blush, this film might seem like an African-American version of *The Wizard of Oz* and, to some, like little more. There are some really interesting things that this film says about the story behind *The Wizard of Oz*, however.

The Wizard of Oz was released during the Great Depression, which was obviously a time when many people likely dreamed that there was some faraway place where things weren't so hard; where the drudgery and hardship of life wasn't so crushing. This film takes place, or at least starts out, in New York City during the 1970s, which was a notoriously tough place to live.

Dorothy Gale in this film, aside from being African-American, really isn't that much different than Dorothy Gale in the 1939 version. She's a girl who dreams of places where she could travel and experience wonder. She's not out in the middle of Kansas farm country like Dorothy, but she's trapped within herself. She's very introverted and doesn't have much to do with the outside world, despite the fact that she lives in one of the biggest cities in the world.

As in the first film, the Munchkins are the ones who tell Dorothy that she needs to go off to see the wizard. When she eventually finds him, the Wicked Witch that she has to kill in this film—Evillene— runs a sweatshop and enslaves the Winkles.

The flying monkeys ride motorcycles and, when the film's Wicked Witch character does get a hold of Dorothy and her friends, she's just as violent and brutal as she is in the original. Rather than throwing a bucket of water on Evillene, Dorothy trips a sprinkler system, dousing Evillene and simply dissolving her, much the same as the Wicked Witch was destroyed in the first film.

The Wiz in this film is a fraud, just like in the original. He was a politician—running for dog catcher, no less—who got blown off course and ended up in Oz. Dorothy manages to make it home with the help of Glinda, except she uses the silver shoes in this rendition, not the ruby slippers.

What's interesting about all this is that, if one takes the story of *The Wizard of Oz* and divorces it of all its period trappings, it still works; and it works very well on top of that. This film shows us an urban version of the story, but the message is still the same.

The message that no one can give you what you already have inside of you, and that anyone who promises as much is a fraud, is still loud and clear in this film. The film also has themes of being happy with what one has and of noticing the value of the world that one lives in, even if it does seem dull at times. New York Dorothy changes as much as does Kansas Dorothy as a result of having to take on some very frightening foes in a strange land.

The music in this film also gives it a nice new twist. It's very 70s sounding and, in fact, the film was released by Motown Productions, so people with a love of the style of music that Motown puts out will probably find a lot to love here.

For die-hard fans of the original, this updating might not quite be what they're looking for, but it's undeniable that there are some very good songs in this film and that the concepts and revisions added to the story are interesting. The budget and production values aren't nearly as high and there certainly isn't the level of innovative filmmaking that we see in the *Wizard of Oz*, but it's worth seeing nonetheless, especially for fans of the Oz universe.

Under the Rainbow (1981)

Director

Steve Rash

Starring

Carrie Fisher

Chevy Chase

Under the Rainbow is a comedy film that stars some very big names from the era, including Chevy Chase and Carrie Fisher. Unfortunately, this film plays into some of the rumors and stereotypes that came from the casting call for the Munchkins. How fans regard this will essentially be a matter of whether or not they find it funny and lighthearted or whether they find that the portrayals of the little people are rife with some of the more unpleasant gags that little people are sometimes involved in.

A Faux Making Of

The plot of this film is basically a variation on the actual story of the making of *The Wizard of Oz*. It's generally not regarded as a great film and is oftentimes regarded as a rather bad film, overall.

The action largely takes place at the Culver City Hotel where the original cast that played the Munchkins were put up during the shooting.

There are some really rather unpleasant moments in this film for those who are sensitive to what little people have to put up with. A bellhop, upon seeing the throng of little people show up remarks that they "all look the same". A little person walks between a man's legs onto an elevator, backed by honking trombones. A man with a dummy tells a little person that he must be from "Dussel-dwarf." A wealthy German woman pats a little person on the head and mistakes him for a child.

One of the little people is involved in an espionage plot that flows along with the plot of all the little people being put up in the hotel together.

Much of the action involving the little people plays on the rumors of hard partying. Essentially, it becomes a sort of cinematic freak show, with little people crawling in dumbwaiters, dishwashers, and making all sorts of mischief and needing to be supervised by the average sized people who are seemingly in charge of them.

There are some scenes that are somewhat redeeming, such as the fencing scene between the German agent—who's a little person— and one of the lead little people who is among the cast of Munchkins. While it's not a great moment, to be sure, the actors do a good job of movie fencing, substituting a kitchen counter and other appliances for the stairways, hallways and other obstacles that movie fencers typically navigate as part of the choreography sequence.

It's a Bit Painful

Taking a look at the lives of the real little people who played the Munchkins and what they put up with in terms of stereotyping, stock roles and the freak show mentality with which society oftentimes regarded them actually makes this film a bit revealing. It's not only the little people who are cast in some ways that will likely be unpleasant for more enlightened viewers.

The Japanese tourists in this film all wear the same white suits, playing into the "they all look the same" stereotype once again. The little people are oftentimes used as props, more or less, with their hijinks in the film sometimes playing into the worst stereotypes of little people.

As the real actors revealed in serious films about the filming of *The Wizard of Oz* in legitimate documentaries such as *We're Off to See the Munchkins*, they've spent a long time fighting back against rumors that they were essentially a bunch of drunk, lewd circus performers. It's been over 70 years since that group of rather talented actors and actresses stayed in the hotel in Culver and rumors such as them being rounded up with butterfly maps still persist; even to this day. This doesn't help in that regard.

There are literally scenes of little people swinging from chandeliers, being as drunk as one can be while still being able to stand and other elements that really do play into some nasty stories and stereotypes.

One reviewer on IMDb rather sums up the types of problems that actors and actresses who played the Munchkins had to deal with, and still have to deal with;

"The Culver Hotel played host to all of the actors who played munchkins during the filming of The Wizard of Oz. Apparently, it was a debacle. The actors partied, drank, and wreaked havoc on the hotel during a stay that has become legendary in Los Angeles." Source IMDb

Actually, they didn't, as we've seen, but this is indicative of such prejudice little people have been working hard to fight against for decades. The rumors of their partying and debauchery are, essentially, only considered amusing by some people because of the freak show mentality of it all. Some of the little people do manage to help the protagonists catch the bad guys, which is a nice touch, but, overall, this is one that people who don't want to see the Munchkins disparaged may want to avoid.

There are times when it's mildly amusing, there are times when it just gets tedious and there are times when it's downright insulting.

If you want to know what it was like being one of the Munchkins during the filming of *The Wizard of Oz*, watch one of the documentaries where they interview the real little people who did the work on the film or pick up any of the fine books written about the event. You'll receive better information and you'll walk away with a feeling of respect for the fact that over 100 people went to California, many of them with no acting experience at all, and managed to portray some of the most memorable and beloved characters in film history. This film really doesn't pay any sort of tribute to that and, one has to imagine, had it been more true to real life, it could have included the spy plot as an element of historical fiction and still been a lot funnier if the characters—particularly the little people—had been portrayed more realistically and more respectfully.

To add one more element to this film that just makes it hard to watch, most of the Munchkins run around in their Munchkin costumes.

This film endeavors to be a comedy but, like many comedies that trade in stereotypes—sometimes unwittingly, ignorance is not the same as hate—it's cringe worthy most of the time. If you want to see what little people put up with, you might want to check out *Under the Rainbow* for educational purposes. If you want to see a little person in a great comedic role, check out Danny Woodburn in his *Seinfeld* appearances, which show you can be respectful and have fun at the same time and that good actors who happen to be little people can pull off comedy with a touch of genius without ever getting into this sort of unpleasant territory. Unsurprisingly, this film currently has a 0% rating on Rotten Tomatoes.

Return to Oz (1985)

Director

Walter Murch

Starring

Nicol Williamson

Jean Marsh

Piper Laurie

If you were enchanted by the mystical, fantasy surroundings of Oz in *The Wizard of Oz*, this film is not likely what you're looking for. If you're looking for something that's very close to the vision in Baum's books, however, this film should fit the bill perfectly.

The plot of this film picks up not long after Dorothy's first adventure. Less than a year later, Dorothy wishes she was back in Oz and, as far as this narratives go, the "no place like home" line doesn't really apply to her.

Instead of being transported to the magical land via an errant tornado, she ends up getting back to Oz with the help of her friends. Unfortunately, before she gets back, she's sent to Dr. Worley for a type of electrotherapy treatment designed to help with her persistent melancholy.

Dorothy finds a glyph, escapes the clutches of Dr. Worley, falls in a river in the process and, after being knocked out and waking up, ends up right back in Oz. Her entry into the land is quite a bit bleaker than it was in the original. Rather than being welcomed by the Munchkins as a hero, she finds that instead, they aren't there. The Yellow Brick Road has been torn up and everyone she knew has been turned into stone.

Dorothy's companion in this film isn't Toto, but a talking chicken named Billina. The two have to hide from some very sinister antagonists called the Wheelers, who are basically people who are, as the name implies, provided with wheels instead of feet and hands.

Her companions in this film are Tik-Toc, a clockwork man and Jack Pumpkinhead who, you guessed it, has a pumpkin for a head.

This film introduces a new line of characters, but is noticeably absent of any major Munchkin characters. The main antagonist is the Nome king. Like *The Wizard of Oz*, the characters that Dorothy encounters in Oz are mirrors of people that she knows in real life.

Dorothy manages to save her friends, including the Scarecrow, and to return Princess Ozma to her throne. Once again, she wakes up after a traumatic experience to find herself back in Kansas. The doctor that had been treating her, who was also the Nome king, turns out to have been killed in a fire. The nurse who had pursued her is arrested and carted away.

Dorothy sees her friends from Oz in her mirror, but they tell her that she has to keep Oz a secret. At the end of the film, she goes outside to spend some time with Toto.

Darker and Bleaker

Where the original *The Wizard of Oz* was, for the most part, a fantasy that had a few nightmarish elements here and there but was bright and cheery overall, this film is rather dark. Particularly for younger children, some of the content might be a bit over the top in how disturbing it is. People turned into statues and ornaments, people who have wheels for hands and feet and the overwhelming sense of dread in this film make it more of a journey into a nightmare than a journey into a dream.

For true fans of the Oz mythology, however, this will add a bit of depth to the story. There's more of a sense of real peril here. However dark it may be, it's hard to beat the original Wicked Witch of the West for pure chills, so fans of the original film who liked it for its more twisted elements might miss her presence in this adaptation.

Dr. Worley is played by Nicol Williamson, who is widely regarded as one of the finest actors of his time. Fans of his will likely enjoy seeing him in this role.

We're Off to See the Munchkins Documentary (1993)

Director

John Fricke & John J. Anderson

Starring

Jerry Maren

Nels Nelson

Margaret Pellegrini

Ruth Duccini

Meinhardt Raabe

This is a documentary production that provides some of the best and most reliable information around about the production of *The Wizard of Oz* from the actors and actresses who played the Munchkins. However, because it was made long after the film, not many of the Munchkins were still around at the time that it was made. Some of the most memorable interviews you'll find anywhere are to be found in this film, however.

Information Given

If you're an Oz aficionado, and a fan of the Munchkins in particular, this film is one you'll want to see. It's shot in traditional documentary format, interspersing scenes from the film with interviews with the actors and additional information given by the host.

The documentary offers some excellent information in terms of dispelling some of the most pernicious myths surrounding the Munchkins, and that information has been relied upon, in part, as source material for the information presented here. Jerry Maren, Nels Nelson, Lewis Croft and Margaret Pellegrini are all featured and provide a lot of information on how they were recruited for the film, what working on the set was like and how it drastically affected their lives afterward.

For most people, an opportunity to see the performers who played the Munchkins is not likely to happen, unless they're fortunate enough to meet Jerry Maren. The film shows convention footage, allowing the audience to get a look at the fandom behind Oz and how the performers who played the Munchkins interacted with—and were adored by—the fans who remembered them for their roles.

This film is available on VHS format at present. For fans of the Oz universe who can get a copy of it, it's not going to disappoint you. It's one of the few pieces of work on *The Wizard of Oz* that focuses so exclusively on the Munchkin characters and the actors and actresses who played them. In doing so, it provides a fresh perspective and a lot of new information that even the most dedicated fans won't know, making it well worth seeking out.

The Muppets Wizard of Oz (2005)

Director

Kirk R. Thatcher

Starring

Ashanti

David Alan Grier

Queen Latifah

Quentin Tarantino

Jeffrey Tambor

Just as the name says, this is a version of the *Wizard of Oz* that features the Muppets. The story is changed around quite a bit from the original, but it's still more or less along the lines of the original *Wizard of Oz* film in terms of a young girl being thrust into a strange land and following her dreams.

A Singer from a Trailer Park

In this film, Dorothy Gale wants to be a singer. She comes from modest roots, living in a trailer park, and her parents don't think that her dreams are realistic. That changes when she finds out that the Muppets are looking for a new singer for their act. She goes to audition but shows up too late to perform. She gives the production team a demo, however.

A tornado hits her trailer park and Dorothy gets caught in it. Instead of a dog, however, she has a pet prawn and he goes along for the ride, as well.

They wake up in Munchkinland, but the Munchkins in this case are rats. The Witches of Oz, both good and evil, are Miss Piggy.

Dorothy gets some magic slippers—silver, this time—and heads off to Oz, not to get home, but to make her dream of becoming a singer a reality.

She meets up with Muppet version of the same companions that Dorothy Gale had in *The Wizard of Oz*. The Cowardly Lion, the Tin Thing and the Scarecrow accompany her on her journey. The story is derivative of the first, but has its own twists, such as the Poppy Field being a club rather than an actual field of poppies.

The four make it to the Emerald City and are told by the Wizard to come back with the eye of the Wicked Witch of the West, rather than her broom.

The Wicked Witch initially wants to send some different minions after Dorothy and her gang, but has to substitute the flying monkeys when the other minions prove unwilling to do the task. Interestingly, the minions that the Miss Piggy version wants to send out are actually closer to the book than they are in the 1939 movie.

Dorothy gets caught, but the Munchkins show up and prevent the Wicked Witch from killing Dorothy.

Quentin Tarantino makes an appearance, inventing all sorts of very Tarantino-ish ways to get rid of the Witch, but he and Kermit decide that a simple kick will do. Dorothy melts the Witch in a bathtub and recovers her eye.

The group heads back to the Emerald City with their prize. Like the original, the Wizard turns out to be humbug, but he comes through on his promise to give them what they want. Dorothy gets her dream of becoming a singer.

Of course, there's no place like home and Dorothy wants to head back soon enough. She uses magic to get there and, upon returning, finds out that the real Muppets actually liked her demo and wanted to hire her. She ends up getting her wish in the real world, too, and the film ends.

A Fun Updating

It's hard not to like the Muppets and this film has a lot of fun with the Oz story. The addition of Quentin Tarantino to the story is particularly funny and makes for some of the best dialogue.

The film really doesn't do anything radical with the story, other than making Dorothy a singer. The Wizard is largely the same, being a regular man with some fancy special effects to make him seem like more than is really the case.

This film may be a fun way to introduce kids to *The Wizard of Oz*, as it doesn't have quite the edge the original does in terms of some of the scares. Though the film may be over 75 years old, The Wicked Witch of the West still has the power to scare kids pretty well, so this might be a nice starting point for them.

Adults, as always, will likely appreciate the way that the writers of Muppet films manage to get some good jokes for adults into the script while still keeping it child friendly. The trailer park setting may also be more relatable for modern kids, who could well find the farm origins of Dorothy Gale in the original to be completely foreign to them.

Overall, it's a good, enjoyable time which is completely appropriate for kids and the Munchkins in this film are particularly funny and a great new way to show them.

Wicked (2003)

Music and Lyrics

Stephen Schwartz

Wicked is a Broadway musical that tells the story of the witches of the land of Oz. It deviates from *The Wizard of Oz* in showing the Wicked Witch of the West, called Elphaba in this production, as a sympathetic character and one far more complex than the villain as portrayed in the 1939 film. It's based on the book *Wicked The Life and Times of the Wicked Witch of the West* by Gregory Maguire.

The Basics of Wicked

Wicked paints a much more complex picture of Oz than we see in *The Wizard of Oz*. Rather than a fantasy land created in the mind of a little girl who falls off a fence, this film shows us a land populated by the same exotic and magical characters, but one that is also very much like the real world. There are plenty of intrigues, betrayals and alliances that come into play throughout the film and the Wicked Witch of the West is certainly not the most nefarious character around.

The Munchkins play a part in this film, being oppressed by various characters and restricted to staying in their native Munchkinland. They are shown as sympathetic characters in this production, as well. But Galinda—the name used for the Glinda in this production—is as much a part of their oppression as anyone else.

This is a retelling of the story that's updated and given more of an adult feel. For those audiences that primarily love *The Wizard of Oz* for its fairytale elements, this production may not appeal to them as much as the original, though it has received excellent reviews and the music and characters are interesting and have some real depth to them.

The Wizard of Oz himself is something of a villain in this film, turning out to be the father of the Wicked Witch of the West. Dorothy and her crew are, essentially, a hit squad, but Dorothy's famous melting of the witch turns out to be a ruse in this production.

Galinda heads back to Oz to be part of the power structure and the Wicked Witch of the West, misunderstood entirely, takes off with her true friend.

You'll probably get to like the Wicked Witch of the West in this play. Particularly interesting is the story of the Scarecrow, which uses a great plot twist to completely flip the script around.

Tin Man (2007)

Director

Nick Willing

Starring

Zoe Deschanel

Neal McDonough

Alan Cumming

Kathleen Robertson

Tin Man is a miniseries, running over four hours, that was produced by the Sci Fi Channel and that aired during December of 2007. It significantly updates *the Wizard of Oz* story, giving it a lot of darker twists but also injecting some humor into it that resonated well with audiences. This miniseries was an award winner, taking home an Emmy for its efforts.

A Modern Oz

Dorothy in this film is referred to as DG, the initials of Dorothy Gale. She works at a restaurant in Kansas and is a grown up, rather than a child as in the original. She has premonitions of a coming storm.

In this film, DG is not transported to Oz via a random tornado, but when the evil queen of O.Z.—the word is an acronym for "Outer Zone" in this story—sends her troopers after DG.

DG manages to survive the storm and ends up in O.Z. She meets up with the Scarecrow character, called Glitch in this rendition, who is only missing part of his brain in this film. The Tin Man in this film was a police officer. When DG discovers him, he was locked in an iron prison shaped like a man where he was forced to relive a traumatic event over and over again. Her third companion is Raw, who possesses psychic powers.

The Queen, Azkadellia, is as frightening as the Wicked Witch in this film, though far more beautiful. DG goes on her quest, finding out that her real mother was from O.Z. and that the parents who were raising her in Kansas were some kind of robots.

Toto is in this film, as well, but he's a man who is able to shape shift into a dog. The group goes up against Azkadellia, trying to pry loose her brutal hold on O.Z.

In this film, the plot doesn't center on Dorothy's quest to get back home but to stop Azkadellia's plot to permanently plunge O.Z. into darkness. DG finds out that her mother was a queen and the first person to travel between Dorothy's world and O.Z.

Azkadellia turns out to be a friend from DG's childhood who was possessed by the spirit of an evil witch. Dorothy manages to break the spell and is quickly restored to her former, good, self.

Darker and More Modern

Tin Man essentially dispenses with the more childlike feel of *The Wizard of Oz* and transforms it into a film that's really intended for adults. It's not full of musical numbers and the lollipops, lullabies and other trappings of a child's dream world are absent from it. In fact, it's quite a dark story, but it definitely has its merits.

For those who are fascinated by the world that Baum created and who want to see it realized in a grittier, more thrilling way, this miniseries is definitely worth taking a look at. Some of the interesting changes include transforming the Wicked Witch's flying monkey minions from winged monkeys to mobats, which are tattooed on Askadellia's collarbones as well as across her sternum. When she needs them, they fly out from her, and are just as horrifying as the flying monkeys in the original film.

There's also an interesting update here in terms of the conventions that were in place in the 1930's versus where they stand today. As an example, Dorothy's checkered dress, in this version, is the uniform that DG wears at work, but she opts for pants and a short jacket when she's adventuring around O.Z.

Likewise, Glitch, the Tin Man and Toto are all updated. Glitch isn't someone who was born without a brain but someone who had half of his brain removed by Azkadellia. He's got a zipper in his head to show for it. The Tin Man is a no-nonsense cop type with an appropriately Wild West name, Wyatt Cain. His name derives from both his punishment and the badge that he wore as a lawman.

Azkadellia, essentially the Wicked Witch of the West, is not portrayed as ugly, which was a common convention for identifying characters as evil in the era of *The Wizard of Oz*. In this film, she's actually quite beautiful, oddly giving her the air of being even more dangerous than the old crone who appeared in the first film.

Particularly for fans of films that don't mind blending science and magic together, *Tin Man* is worth seeing. You won't find the merry, pleasant Munchkins here to comfort you when you arrive, but the sense of danger is very real and, when Azkadellia gets wicked, one does well to watch out.

Oz the Great and Powerful (2011)

Director

Sam Raimi

Starring

James Franco

Mila Kunis

Rachel Weisz

Michelle Williams

This film isn't quite a prequel to *The Wizard of Oz* but, as the name implies, it's very much related. This film tells the story of how the Wizard of Oz got to be the Wizard of Oz and has some strong parallels to the 1939 film, with some callbacks to that film found throughout its run time. There are Munchkins in this film and they're actually a bigger part of the action than they were in the first film.

This Time, It's Real

Going back to the 1939 *The Wizard of Oz*, one remembers that the studio executives didn't think that audiences of the time would buy that Dorothy went off to some fantasy land over the rainbow. This is why she wakes up back in sepia-toned Kansas with of all the people who she knew before and in different forms in Oz.

This film takes a different tact; Oz is real. The protagonist is Oz himself, played by James Franco, who works as a circus performer. He's taken to Oz in much the same fashion as Dorothy, getting caught up in a tornado while flying in a hot air balloon. He finds himself in Oz at the end of the tornado journey.

Like *The Wizard of Oz,* the film transitions to color once he gets to Oz. Interestingly, the film also changes from primitive sound to full-on surround once he arrives to the magical land, offering a somewhat updated touch to the entire transition effect.

In this film, Oz meets three witches, one of whom ends up becoming the Wicked Witch of the West, but who starts out as Theodora, a sweet woman played by Mila Kunis who turns wicked because she's suffering from a broken heart. Oz's companions include a flying monkey who, in a significant departure from some of the most frightening characters in the first film, is a good guy.

He also has friends who include Munchkins. As in the first film, they greet him with a song celebrating who he is. They live under the protection of Glinda, just as they did in the first film, though the Wicked Witch of the East isn't tormenting them as of yet.

There is a Wicked Witch from the start in this film, and she killed the King of Oz. The denizens of Oz believe that Oz the man is a prophesized individual who will take out the Wicked Witch for them.

The real Wicked Witch in this film isn't who Oz initially sets out to destroy, namely Glinda. Instead, it's Evanora, who is also responsible for turning Theodora into the Wicked Witch of the West.

Oz ends up leading the Munchkins and other denizens of Oz into battle against the evil Wicked Witch. His friends include the aforementioned flying monkey and a china doll that had her entire village destroyed by the Wicked Witch. Oz manages to fix her, foreshadowing his abilities in *The Wizard of Oz*.

As is the case in *The Wizard of Oz*, Oz the man is a master of illusion, but actually has no real magical powers. He figures out a way to project his face to the Wicked Witches in huge proportions, again much like he does in the 1939 film. It's enough to put a scare into them, particularly when they realize that they cannot harm the projection, as they believe that it is his real form.

Oz manages to drive away the Wicked Witches using his trickery. He sets himself up as the Wizard of Oz, maintaining the illusion. Mirroring what he does in the second film, he gives everyone who helped him a gift that helps them overcome their weaknesses. Knuck, a particularly surly Munchkin who proves to be a loyal friend, receives a mask etched with a happy face on it.

Good Munchkin Callbacks

If you're particularly fond of the Munchkins, this film will likely work for you. Knuck is a great character and he's portrayed in a way that appeals more to the sensibilities of modern viewers, which eliminates some of the more cringe worthy portrayals that you'll see in other renditions. The singing and dancing number should make those who enjoyed the Munchkins in the first movie quite happy as well.

The film stays close to the Oz that was represented in Baum's books, so those who are very much invested in it should find it to be satisfying in that regard, as well.

This film gives some interesting background into the origins of Oz the man and, given that *The Wizard of Oz* is such an established classic, it builds on a story that most people will readily understand. The various Ozite groups shown here include the Tinkers and the Winkles and more. Despite the silly names, there's a bit of darkness in the Oz stories and this film doesn't shy away from it.

Some critics have criticized the CGI effects as being a bit unrealistic at times. Of course, the original film had its moments that were obviously special effects, as well, but this is a fantasy land, after all, and it's easy enough to suspend disbelief long enough to thoroughly enjoy the film.

As far as *Wizard of Oz* related films go, this is one of the better ones and it gives the audience an interesting Munchkin character that's much more a part of the plot than the Munchkins in the original film were.

Chapter 7

Oz Fandom

There are some films and stories out there that end up attracting a huge following. Something about them makes them more compelling than average. Presented with a fantasy world, some people become lost in it and it becomes a sort of part of them, which is how *The Wizard of Oz* has evolved over the years. Taking a look at the books and the original film, as well as those that followed it, it's easy enough to see why.

The Munchkins were only one of many magical races of creatures to be found in Oz, but they've become among the most easily identified and, of course, are renowned fan favorites. In this chapter, we'll take a look at the fandom surrounding the Oz books and films, the conventions that are held to celebrate it, and how the Munchkins became a part of that fandom.

There's a bit of a bittersweet element in this in that only one of the original Munchkin players remains. While Oz fandom will almost certainly endure when all of the original cast and crew are gone, that first film has a significant part in this fandom and, in fact, is really the central focus of much of it.

How the Fandom Started

When exploring Oz fandom, it's important to keep in mind that it took a considerable amount of time for it to gain any real traction. As was revealed in earlier chapters, *The Wizard of Oz*, though it received a great deal of praise from critics, didn't manage to break even on its colossal budget during its first release. It wouldn't do so until it was rereleased again in 1949.

That second release netted the film another $1.5 million at the box office, but it still wasn't that big of a take for a film that cost so much to produce. While *The Wizard of Oz* is best appreciated on a movie screen, given its scale and the spectacular use of color, it came into its own on the small television screens that started popping up in homes across America during the 1950s.

There's something quite interesting about this. One of the most appealing elements of *The Wizard of Oz* is the way it uses color to differentiate the real world from the Land of Oz. On an early television, of course, the entire film would be in black and white for the vast majority of viewers. Those lucky enough to have color televisions could see it in all its glory, however. Some stores even allowed families to come into their shops and watch the film in glorious color.

The Television Showings

In the 1950s, people started buying televisions and, of course, that meant that broadcasters had to come up with material to keep audiences watching those screens. Most television shows of the time were live-action affairs, but there was room for films. In 1956, CBS broadcasted *The Wizard of Oz* over the airwaves for the first time ever.

The first broadcast, according to the Oz Wiki, pulled in 44 million viewers. It only got better after that. It would be three years until the film was broadcast over the airwaves again and the audience naturally grew.

Following that second broadcast, the film became an annual event on television, much like the animated Christmas specials and other family fare that were broadcast on a yearly basis by the networks.

This carried on throughout the 20th Century, usually with a host presenting the film to give information or to just tout the importance of the film culturally and to film history. Some broadcasts featured documentaries on the making of the film to go along with the showing.

There were even incidents where the film was preempted, consequently garnering angry responses from viewers.

By 1999, the film had migrated from broadcast networks to cable television. This changed the broadcasts, and the schedule of broadcasts, remarkably. Rather than being a yearly event, the film was shown much more frequently, oftentimes without any of the fanfare that accompanied the broadcast showings of the film.

Releases and Rereleases

According to the same source, the total television sales for the film had gone up to a whopping $34.5 million by 1988. In the 1980s, VHS and Betamax players were widely available and 850,000 video tapes of the film were sold, netting another $16.7 million for the film.

The film has appeared in different incarnations over the years. For instance, the release of the film in 1989 for the VHS market substituted standard black and white for the sepia tone Kansas sequences of the original, which some fans found objectionable.

The film has also had its aspect ratio changed and even been released in IMAX 3D. The 75th Anniversary Edition of the film was a huge event, with the film being shown at the renovated Grauman's Chinese Theater to commemorate the original release, which, of course, didn't occur there, but instead at smaller theaters a few days before.

The film is currently available in Blu-Ray format, the most advanced format on the market at this time. It has been released in every other format for home viewers along the way. It's also available for streaming over the Internet, as this option has gradually been gaining in popularity for most films and, of course, there's always demand for *The Wizard of Oz*. The film has even been "riffed" by the Rifftrax comedy troupe.

With the film being available in so many formats and so popular, it's managed to maintain a very large fan base and to see that fan base continually grow.

Heading to Oz

Films that have large fan bases are very rarely standalone affairs. For instance, *Star Trek, Star Wars, The Lord of the Rings, Dune* and other franchises that have spawned very active groups of fans who celebrate those films typically have many books and other media associated with them. *The Wizard of Oz*, of course, is based on a book that is but one in a very large series of books. As we explore the fandom that surrounds this film, we'll see that many of the fans are deeply involved in the mythology that Baum created. *The Wizard of Oz*, however, is oftentimes the metaphorical Yellow Brick Road that first leads fans to their new found obsession, and the film is oftentimes the main focus of these fan events.

Understanding the world that Baum created takes a bit of work, but it also makes it apparent why people identify so strongly with the characters and places that are portrayed in the book.

The Fan Gatherings and the Munchkin Presence

As was noted in prior chapters, the actors and actresses who played the Munchkins found themselves very much welcome presences at the various events held around the nation to commemorate Baum and his books. Of course, for most people, the way that they even became familiar with Oz was through the 1939 movie, given that it's essentially an institution, at this point.

International Wizard of Oz Club Convention

The largest events held to commemorate Oz and his writings oftentimes feature many references to the Munchkins. When more of the original actors and actresses who played them in *The Wizard of Oz* were alive, some lucky fans got to see them in person. Today, that's all but impossible, but their presence is still very much felt globally.

The International Wizard of Oz Club Convention is held yearly in Baum's hometown of Chittenango, New York. Look at the list of events and you'll quickly see how much the Munchkins are a part of the entire mythology.

There's a Munchkin Tour during the event. There's a Munchkin Mile Fun Run. There's even a tribute page on the group's website dedicated to the Munchkins, which currently has an obituary for Karl Slover. As the obituary notes, he was one of the fortunate actors who managed to enjoy popularity for his role in *the Wizard of Oz* later in life and there's some very touching writing about the man on the site.

The International Wizard of Oz Club also publishes a magazine called the Baum Bugle, which focuses on Oz and its inhabitants. It is available through their site and has been published since the 1950s. It's gone from a mimeographed newsletter to a full-fledged magazine, complete with a color cover, over the years.

Indiana Wizard of Oz Festival

Across the nation, *The Wizard of Oz* remains a reason for people to gather together and share their love of the film. The Indiana Wizard of Oz Festival has the Munchkinland Market Days as part of their events. A look at their hall of fame shows how much the performers who played the Munchkins added to the proceedings, with Slover, Rabbe, Pellegrini, Mary Ellen St. Aubin and Jerry and Elizabeth Maren featured in images on the sites.

Autumn at Oz Festival

Head to Beech Mountain, NC and you can take in the Autumn at Oz Festival. This event is held in October and gives visitors a chance to see a theme park that was designed exclusively to recreate the magical land. The theme park was severely damaged in a fire, but it opens its gates once per year and those who want to experience what Oz might have been like can enjoy the event, meet the characters and see recreations of some of Baum's fantasy landscapes.

OZtoberFest

Of course, Kansas was Dorothy's home state and, as she said, there's no place like home. Every year, Wamego, KS has the OZtoberFest, where people gather over the weekend to celebrate the film and its lasting legacy.

Again, look at the page for the site and you'll see the actors who played the Munchkins right on the first page. The event features attractions such as the Oz Winery, a museum that has, according to the site, the largest privately owned collection of memorabilia related to the film and even Toto's Tacoz, which also features Munchkins Tacoz on the menu.

The Museum, however, is particularly worth noting.

The Oz Museum in Wamego

According to the Oz Museum site, this museum was made possible by a grant from the State of Kansas. To turn that money into a real museum, members of the community of Wamego volunteered their time to put it all together.

The museum has in excess of 2,000 different items that relate to *The Wizard of Oz* and the world that Baum created. It includes everything from board games to collectables to items related to other films that take place in the Oz universe. The museum has hosted podcasts and other events to promote the story and the film and, for those who really want to dig deep into the history of the film and Oz on the whole, it's a great place to visit and intrepidly explore. The fact that the festival is held in the same town only makes that easier to do.

Winkie Con, Oz Con International

The Winkies live in the western part of Oz and that means that, when conventions take place on the West Coast, keeping in the proper Oz spirit means giving these former serfs of the Wicked Witch of the West their due. You'll find all the other Oz characters given proper recognition at this convention as well, of course, and plenty of entertaining things to do.

Winkie Con started up in 1964. The goal of the convention is to both provide a way for fans to get together and enjoy the mythology but, also, to foster rather serious research into Baum, his books and the world that he created within their covers.

This is the longest running of all the annual Oz events. Those who want to get into the world of Oz will find plenty of opportunities to do so here, and there is usually an impressive lineup of guests who come to discuss *The Wizard of Oz*, the books from which it was derived and associated other works.

Chapter 8

The Cultural Impact of *The Wizard of Oz*

The cultural impact of *The Wizard of Oz* is something that should not be underestimated. The roles of the Munchkins provided little people with a unique role in film, which allowed them to break out of roles that were disparaging, disrespectful and that played on their size as a way to get cheap laughs or public sympathy. While those roles still do occur and while many little people who work as actors and actresses still have to contend with them, it's hard to deny that the Munchkin roles were among the first times that little people appeared in a role that really portrayed them as equals to those who were around them. They weren't lesser human beings. They were good people who got liberated by an innocent girl and her errant, flying house.

There's far more to *The Wizard of Oz* in terms of its cultural impacts, however. There are some that are so universal and common that it's easy to forget where they came from. Let's look at a few.

Dorothy's Journey

When Dorothy meets the Munchkins, she's enchanted and somewhat confused, and understandably so. She's in a dream world of sorts, but it's not a dream world where everything is as friendly as the Lollipop Guild or any of the other very kindhearted Munchkins she meets. Conversely, the danger is very real in this world.

Some writers find significant symbolism in this, and it's not too difficult to see. Let's look at some of the ways that this story can be interpreted. Once one digs a bit deeper into this iconic film, it's obvious that there are some elements to its story that are universal and others that are very American.

Childhood to Adult

One of the most common interpretations of *The Wizard of Oz* is that it represents the journey from childhood to adulthood that we all go through. The Munchkins are at the beginning of this journey. They're all lullabies and lollipops and their childlike stature emphasizes that. They wear colorful clothing, speak in friendly, non-threatening voices and Dorothy finds herself smack in the middle of them when she arrives to Oz.

The Munchkins prepare Dorothy for her journey. They fill her with confidence by greeting her as a hero. They tell her how to get where she has to go and then send her on her way with warm wishes. For a child of Dorothy's age, leaving this safe little village would be a very hard thing to do, but the Wicked Witch of the West shows up and gives her the impetus to do so. She might be in a beautiful, friendly place, but it's time to head off and see what the world has to offer and, in fact, to take on its worst aspects and conquer them.

Her journey takes her through a place that is both enchanting and terrifying. Her companions represent what she'll need to complete this journey. She'll need brains, courage and a strong heart. Like the people she travels with, her journey shows her that, all along, she had all three; she just needed to be tested to prove to herself that she could take on the things that scared her, all in her quest to find her way home.

She journeys from the innocent and beautiful world of the Munchkins to the metropolis of The Emerald City. She's given a mission and, again, has to overcome her fears and conquer the Wicked Witch of the West. Not only does she have to conquer the Witch, she has to get her broom, which is no small feat in itself. Though this may be a tale written for children, the Wicked Witch has some truly terrifying powers, even for an adult.

Dorothy is scared, and understandably so. When her friends come to rescue her, however, and when the Wicked Witch sets her friend the Scarecrow on fire, Dorothy stops being a scared girl and takes action, even if she's not clear that she's just launched an attack that will take the Wicked Witch out for good. She famously melts her with a bucket of water, saving her friends and her own life in the process.

It's after that the Oz, who is exposed for being a fraud, gives her friends at least symbolic representations of the brains, heart and courage they've all been after. They had it all along, of course, but they needed it to be acknowledged; some kind of milestone. Glinda tells Dorothy that she just needs to click her heels and say that there's no place like home and she'll be off. Dorothy realizes how much she'll miss her friends and gives them an emotional goodbye before heading off to Kansas again.

There's a lot of symbolism here. Like anyone making the transition from childhood to adult, Dorothy has to leave a world where nonthreatening people treat her with warmth, decency and kindness and enter a world where she has very real, and very dangerous, enemies. She has to take a road that, while she may know where it ends, she doesn't know the path through which it will lead her. She has to go from a little girl who needs protection to someone who can fight her own battles, and win them, and do so even when she's afraid for her very life. She has to find it in herself to fight back, even when it seems certain that she's outmatched and, in fact, when she is outmatched.

When she leaves Oz, she realizes the world she's leaving behind is something to which she may never return. She knows she'll miss it and she knows that the real world is one that is far less colorful and one that is certainly not enchanted and magical. It's a world where her enemies may be more mundane, but where they're real threats, nonetheless. It's a world where people toil in dusty barnyards and fields. There's no place like it, however, and one gets the sense that, however hard and uneventful life on Dorothy's Kansas farm may have been, there is no place like it and Dorothy will likely look back on it fondly as an adult.

Dorothy's hardships make her what she is, and her trials and tests are inevitable part of her becoming an adult. For a generation that was living through the Great Depression, there must have been something here that really struck a chord. What makes this film so remarkable is that, even for several generations after the Greatest Generation, this movie still *continued* to strike a chord.

Urbanization and The Frontier

It's easy to forget that the frontier era didn't end too long before the 1939 version of *The Wizard of Oz* was filmed. People who lived as Dorothy's family did, out on the plains in farm country, were far outside the rapidly developing urban landscapes of the east and west coasts.

For some, there is a great deal of symbolism that relates to the way that Americans of the time perceived themselves and their changing world to be found in this film.

The urbanization of the US had profound political implications, of course, and they are viewed by some to be on full display in this film. Dorothy, for instance, can be seen to represent traditional values, or seen to be on a a quest for them. The characters around her are extensions of this. She's on a quest to find her home again and has to exhibit courage, heart and intelligence to do so. Some writers find Toto to be representative of the average person, and he's the one who actually exposes the Wizard as humbug.

The Munchkins, in this interpretation, are also seen to represent average people. They are good, kind and rather innocent, in ways, and are—until Dorothy's house crushes the witch—oppressed by appalling wickedness.

To fully understand the political interpretations of this film—more so the book from which it's derived—one needs to delve into some arcane elements of economics and to realize that some of the parts of the movie that diverge from the film were actually rewritten to show off the true glory of Technicolor.

About Those Shoes

While *The Wizard of Oz* is associated with the Great Depression, there was another depression that preceded it in the late 1800s. The book was published in 1900, meaning that its ties to monetary policy—they are there, believe it or not—are tied to the politics of that era. The following theory was developed by Henry Littlefield, a high school teacher, and was neatly outlined by the BBC.

During the late 1800s, the US was on the Gold Standard. Under this system, the value of the dollar was tied to the amount of gold which was available to back the dollar. The Populists, a political movement, represented farmers and laborers who wanted to change the gold standard and to use silver as a standard.

Farmers and laborers were struggling with tremendous debt burdens at this time. Adding a silver standard would have ended a deflationary economic condition that led to their debt becoming even more significant over time. It's all rather arcane, particularly in an era where the Gold Standard is about as relevant as crank-start cars, but it does play a part in this story.

"Oz" is an abbreviation for "ounce", the measure by which gold is valued. The Wizard himself represents presidential power. The Scarecrow is a farmer, the Tin Man a laborer and Dorothy is the everyday person. The Cowardly Lion represents William Jennings Bryan in this interpretation, who backed the silver standard but, in the end, turned out to have no real power or influence.

The Yellow Brick Road is, of course, made of gold, and it represents the Gold Standard. Dorothy doesn't have ruby slippers in the original novel. She has a pair of silver shoes. Of course, everything in black in white films can be interpreted as silver, so the red slippers were added to show off the color sequences of the film.

Dorothy's journey in this interpretation is a metaphor for how gold and silver together will lead her back home, to her farm, a symbol of the US at the time. She takes the Yellow Brick Road to Oz—which is Washington DC in this interpretation—and reaches the seat of power, the president. Of course, the city is Emerald or, to put it in less attractive language, it's green like money. When she gets there, the power behind the city is exposed to be a complete fraud, a not-too-subtle critique of the presidents who had previously backed the Gold Standard.

Interestingly, in the book, Dorothy loses her silver shoes in the desert.

It's both gold and silver—which was the goal of the Free Silver Movement—that make everything right again, however.

This doesn't transform the story into some radical manifesto and, according to this interpretation, it's merely an allegory for what was going on politically at the time, not an endorsement of any particular side in the debate. There's also no real proof that Baum was a Populist. Nonetheless, it does make everything seem a bit less magical.

The Munchkins fit neatly into this interpretation, as they are kind and innocent but oppressed by forces that they don't really understand, and who they cannot really stand up to realistically. The travel of the companions to the Emerald City represents this movement making its way to Washington DC.

It's not the most enchanting interpretation but it's interesting. It's also indicative of how long this story has lasted, given that the political issues being discussed according to this interpretation, are so far in the past that most people wouldn't even recognize them these days. However, this theory has some significant backing. At the same time, absent of any political elements, the story has remained one of the most beloved of all time and, once those political considerations were things of the past, one could argue that the best elements of the story were free to rise to the surface. It's a fairy tale these days, a uniquely American one in many regards but still one that can touch anyone who sees it, no matter where they're from in terms of nation or era.

When you're watching *The Wizard of Oz*, it's good to keep in mind that many of the most beloved children's films have elements in them that make them appealing to adults, as well. Taken in this context, *The Wizard of Oz* is important in several ways. There's the political allegory just described and the fact that, when Hollywood started to really evolve in terms of technology, one element of costume, the ruby slippers, took on an entirely other meaning than what may have been originally intended by the author. The ruby slippers, and their bright red color, also represent the era of color film coming into its own.

One Last Element of Symbolism in the Munchkins

One last symbolic interpretation of the Munchkins is really quite compelling. The Lollipop Guild is among the Munchkins who welcome Dorothy to Oz. At the time the book was written, child labor was one of the cruel realities of everyday life. For some, the Lollipop Guild represents child laborers. It's not much of a stretch to see this. They are among the most childlike Munchkins in both appearance and the way that they act. Of course, lollipops themselves are frequently associated with children, so it's no wonder that people made this connection so readily.

Finding Your Own Meaning

Some books and films out there are so potentially broad in their interpretations and profound in their influence that people are motivated to find their own meanings in them. L. Frank Baum's work and the 1939 *The Wizard of Oz* are both examples of such ambiguity.

Whether *The Wizard of Oz* is an interesting film interpretation of a book about gold and silver politics in the 1800s, a story that tells about growing up and losing youth—and then missing it—or something else, it's everyone's to interpret however they wish. There's no right and wrong in any of this.

For little people and people who are interested in learning more about their role in Hollywood, there are some meanings that go beyond metaphor and that are starkly real.

Little people struggled mightily in society at the beginning of the 1900s and still do to deal with prejudice and discrimination. While they may have been underpaid and overworked on *The Wizard of Oz*, they ended up creating something that is undeniable in its importance culturally, to film and to the perception of little people today.

However you may see this film, one would do well to appreciate the Munchkins as more than characters in a film. Of all the representations of little people in film and other entertainment that you'll see from this era, *The Wizard of Oz* is among the most interesting and meaningful, and it did make a genuine difference in the lives of many of the actors and actresses involved.

What About those Costumes, Sets and Other Items?

As we saw in the interviews with the actors who played the Munchkins, even a program from the opening could fetch thousands of dollars among collectors. The other items associated with the film are equally prized treasures among collectors. Some of these items have become iconic in their own right, so they have meaning that goes far beyond the roles that they play in the story.

The Ruby Slippers

Gilbert Adrian came up with the original design for the ruby slippers. There was more than one pair made. The pair that wasn't used had a more ornate style and invoked Arabian influences, with curling toes. They had an overall over-the-top appearance to them that didn't quite fit in with Dorothy's look overall.

After working on designs for a while, they came up with the final design. These are heavily sequined shoes and, according to most reliable sources, six pairs were made in total for the film.

One pair was auctioned off in the 1970s and is now available for viewing in the Smithsonian Institution. This is believed to be the pair that Judy Garland wore during the shooting of the film.

As is the case with most movie props and costume items, there are usually versions made for general use and a version made that has better detail and higher quality that is made specifically for close-up shots. This pair is known as the Witch's Slippers as they were likely the ones used in the scene where Dorothy takes them from the Wicked Witch of the East. Film historians reached this conclusion by comparing the known pairs with the pair that is removed from the Witch in the film. These are also believed to be the ones that Dorothy wears when Glinda tells her to click her heels together to get back home.

There is one other pair that may have been worn by a stunt double, but this is disputed. They are currently in private ownership.

The pair of slippers that are currently in the Smithsonian sold for a whopping $15,000 at auction in the 1970s, giving some indication of how much people are willing to pay for verified, authentic memorabilia from the film.

At the Smithsonian itself, the Ruby Slippers are among the most popular items on exhibit. One retired curator related to the LA Times that more than 5 million people come to the exhibit every single year and that the sheer amount of traffic has resulted in them having to replace the rug in front of the display, or patch it, many times over. Like the Munchkins, the shoes seem to have a particularly strong effect on children, who are drawn to them and oftentimes stand transfixed.

Interestingly, the Smithsonian, because it cannot be verified to a reasonable degree, doesn't claim that these are *the* ruby slippers that Judy Garland wore, but does know for sure that they were used during the production. Because there are so many different pairs of shoes from the production, no one may ever know for sure, but people have spent a lot of time trying to figure it out.

According to the Smithsonian itself, one of the alternate pairs of ruby slippers went for $600,000 at auction back in 2000.

The Munchkin Costumes

The Costumes worn by the Munchkins can still fetch a high price and are often sold exclusively between collectors. One of the pairs of pants that went with the original costumes fetched $7,000 on EBay in 2014.

Another Munchkin costume that went up for auction fetched a whopping $9,600 as the final bid. It's labeled with John Leal's name on the inside, an actor who did go on to make public appearances for fans but who also had a career in the aerospace industry. That costume consisted of a long jacket, colored grey, with green lapels and a purple lining. Leal played the parts of both a soldier and a villager in the original production.

Many of the Munchkins who made appearances at festivals wore costumes that were reproductions of their original wardrobe from the film. You can see some of them wearing their costumes on YouTube in a video interview with Newsweek.

The costumes are still used as references by other costume makers because of their unique look. As the article referenced above points out, the Munchkin costumes are clearly made to invoke a specific period, but it's not clear which one. They're also unclear in terms of which nationality they would represent and so forth. This lends the Munchkins, to a great degree, their unique and magical appearance.

The most complete Munchkin costume known is owned by a couple who have, on top of the costume, the largest collection of items from the film known. It was recently on display in Rockwell, Maine and was only displayed once before, in LA in 2000. This collection contains not only the Munchkin costumes, but also the Wicked Witch of the West's hourglass and plenty of other items which are related to the film.

Of course, many of the costumes remain lost to history. At the time when the film was made, old wardrobe and other items related to filming movies was oftentimes simply warehoused or discarded. Some of those items were snatched by workers at the film lots, who knew that the studios really didn't care if the items were stolen from the studios. Of course, that was until it became apparent that collectors are willing to pay thousand—sometimes tens of thousands—of dollars for those items.

Unfortunately, the sets and other elements that made *The Wizard of Oz* what it was are largely gone. While the importance of the film is readily apparent to anyone in today's era, it was a moderate success when it was released and really didn't come into its own until many decades after it was made.

Likewise, the importance of the Munchkins themselves would have been hard to see when the film was first released. Today, however, while all but one of the original actors are gone, their legacy remains one of the most influential for little people and on Hollywood as a whole. The fantastic price that people are willing to pay for authentic memorabilia related to the Munchkins and the genuine affection that people exhibited toward the actors and actresses who gave up their time to attend the conventions is proof of that.

The memorabilia provides a tangible connection to one of the most significant films ever made. Actually getting to meet one of the actors who played the Munchkins certainly would have been a thrill for any fan and, because of that, it's no surprise that they were so popular with fans; both young and old.

If You Want to Collect

If you do want to collect items from *The Wizard of Oz*, it's highly advisable to look into how they can be authenticated before buying. You'll find offers all over the Internet, but remember that the real deal will always cost a lot of money. Finding a Munchkin costume or even something less significant would be a genuine thrill for any fan.

As we can see, Oz has a very dedicated fandom and many conventions. One of these conventions would be a logical starting point, and finding a bona fide expert at one of them shouldn't be too hard.

Chapter 9

All About Oz: Book vs. Film

There's a lot more to Oz than we see in *The Wizard of Oz*. That film is from the first book and, over the years, Baum added a great amount of detail to his land and information to its inhabitants.

It became a mythology, after a time, on the scale and level of other huge franchises that managed to grow in similar ways.

Like many of those franchises and series of books, there are some inconsistencies to be found. The Land of Oz pops up in various places around the world, the history of the land changes now and then and, in some cases, right and left even change. No matter how it's represented in the books and films, however, Oz continues to enchant.

To truly understand the phenomenon that is Oz, one has to look at the books and the expansions on the stories that followed over the years. The first book was written more than 100 years ago, first coming out in 1900 and was intended to be just one book, not part of an expansive series.

Over the years, the people's love of the book and the stories that it tells made it one of the most popular fantasy worlds of all. This is much more than one film. What Baum ended up creating was a place where imaginative children and adults could uncover more and more about his mythical land and where they could identify with strange creatures and peoples who are as memorable as those in the most established fantasy epics in the world.

Hang on tight, because we're headed over the rainbow, and sometimes it's hard for people to figure out whether or not they want to come back once they get there!

Who Are the Munchkins, Really?

Understanding Oz requires that one understands that mistakes sometimes end up creating the most interesting of worlds.

There are varying stories about how this happened, involving everything from misreading and, therefore, misaligning printing plates to editors correcting what they thought was a mistake, but actually wasn't, but Oz doesn't have a consistent East and West direction.

Any fan of the 1939 film knows that the Munchkins were ruled with an iron fist by the Wicked Witch of the East. Logically, Dorothy should have been heading west on the Yellow Brick Road when she went off to see the Wizard. Looking at a map from *Tik-Tok of Oz*, you'll see that the Munchkins are situated to the west of the Emerald City, while the compass rose at the top clearly indicates that the directions are as they would be on a standard map of the real world. In short, the Munchkins are in the wrong place. However, in a map of Oz that comes from radio plays of the stories, the orientation is correct, with the Munchkins located in the east and the Winkies in the west.

There are various retcons that attempt to explain this, but there are other inconsistencies, as well. The Land of Oz is sometimes described as being a part of the Americas, though clouded by magic. In other cases, it appears to be located somewhere in the oceans. In some stories, it's completely surrounded by deserts.

The result, however, doesn't amount to much. While such an inconsistency might drive fans of Tolkien and other authors who have created fantasy lands out of their mind, Oz is all about enchantment and magic, so it doesn't necessarily create much of a problem. For all practical purposes, the Munchkins are located in the eastern part of Oz and lived under the rule of the Wicked Witch of the East, at least until Dorothy dropped a house on her.

The Munchkins that appear in the 1939 version of the film are not precisely like the Munchkins as Baum envisioned them. They are smaller than average, being about the size of a child. They wear only blue, however, and they also wear pointed hats, similar to the hats that the Wicked Witch of the West wears in the film.

The Munchkins in the film, of course, are a colorful bunch and include many different outfits among their wardrobe and have professionals as well as villagers among their troupe. In the novels, each area of Oz had its own color and the Munchkins were blue, as was nearly everything in the area dominated by the Wicked Witch of the East. When Dorothy arrives in the novel, she's wearing both the color of the good witches and the color of the Munchkins, so the Munchkins regard her as a witch herself, and a good one at that.

The consistency between the books and the movie is that Dorothy genuinely liberated the Munchkins from the brutality of the Wicked Witch of the East in both cases. The changes that were made are easy enough to understand. They were showing off the Technicolor process, so the more color that was included, the better.

Because of their childlike size, they remain relatable characters to children. Of course, the little people who played them in the original Wizard of Oz were mostly about the size of a child, making them natural choices for these memorable characters.

In Oz, however, not all of the fantasy creatures particularly care about lollipops and singing pleasant songs. Some of them are downright terrifying.

Baum's mythical land was expanded on by the author in ways that are sometimes quite dark. Let's look at some of the most memorable villains.

The Wicked Witch of the West

Like any great character, not everyone sees the Wicked Witch of the West in the same way. In fact, in *Wicked,* she's a protagonist character. In *Oz, the Great and Powerful*, she's somewhere in between, starting out as a sweet person and gradually becoming corrupted by a far more wicked witch.

In the books, she only appears in the first book, in which she is killed off by Dorothy, just as is the case in the movie. She's the iron-fisted and cruel ruler of Winkie Country. There are some significant differences between her as portrayed in the book and in the movie, however.

In the book, the castle that the Wicked Witch of the West calls home is enough to give even an adult the chills. In the book, it's simply gorgeous. In the film, she laments that Dorothy killed her sister but, in the book, they're both witches and not sisters.

In the books, she not only uses flying monkeys to do her bidding and act as muscle, she also has a swarm of bees, an entire army of her oppressed Winkies, a pack of wolves and crows to back her up.

The Wicked Witch of the West isn't on a quest for revenge in this film. She doesn't care at all about the Wicked Witch of the East getting killed off and is only after Dorothy because she wants to steal her silver shoes.

Her flying monkeys are also not the devoted servants that they're portrayed as in the film. In the books, she has limited power over them and it's because she has a magical hat. She also—just as is the case in the Muppet version of the film—has an eye that allows her to see anything and everything that goes on in Oz.

One of the iconic elements in *The Wizard of Oz* is the broom that the Wicked Witch of the West flies on. As was noted, a stand-in for Hamilton was injured during a special effects sequence that made use of the broom. In the novel, she doesn't even have a broom, but carries an umbrella.

The Wicked Witch of the West in the novels is just as fearsome as she is in the film and, in fact, a bit more so. Everyone is afraid of her, up to and including Glinda and the Wizard himself.

She does have the same fatal weaknesses, however. She's desperately afraid of water, which makes one wonder if there's some reference to being downright rabid in her character. She's also afraid of the dark, oddly enough, which would have made her castle as portrayed in the film a frightening place for her, indeed.

This character has been updated in many different ways to suit the time in which films involving her were made. In *Wicked, Oz the Great and Powerful* and *Tin Man*, she's really a rather sympathetic character. In all of those renditions, she's not evil to the core but, rather, became that way because someone misunderstood her, led her astray or outright possessed her, as is the case in *Tin Man*.

Regardless of she came to be wicked, however, this is one witch that no one wants to tangle with. She's incredibly powerful, practically omniscient in some renditions and, in every telling, cruel in the extreme. She's a very effective representation of outright evil in action and, particularly in the 1939 film, is one of the most famous villains in history.

In all portrayals, except *Wicked*, she is imperial in her nature. She wants to expand her power until she rules the whole of Oz and, as far as the other characters in the stories are concerned, she's powerful enough to make that dream happen.

Winged Monkeys

The Winged Monkeys as they appeared in the 1939 version were enough to test the mettle of any child who saw the film. It's likely that many of us remember seeing them through our fingers, trying to block out their nightmarish visages as best as possible while still watching the film.

In the novels, the monkeys aren't the minions of the Wicked Witch of the West, but are bound to obey the possessor of a gold cap that gives control over them. They have to obey that individual three times.

In the novels, the monkeys aren't all bad, either. They're actually just sort of trickster characters driven to do evil by the Wicked Witch of the West. In fact, they are actually sympathetic characters in the novel.

Glinda eventually proves how good she is by using the cap just twice and then handing it back to the monkeys. Her second order to them is to stop hurting people and then she gives them back their freedom.

Chapter 10

The Art of Oz

The artwork used on the covers of Baum's various Oz books shows signs of the times in which they were made. Some of the characters very much resemble the movie characters and others are far flung from what appear in the 1939 film.

John R. Neil

John R. Neil is probably the artist most associated with L. Frank Baum's Oz universe more than any other. In total, he illustrated in excess of forty different stories that took place in Oz. These include stories written by Baum himself and stories which were written by other authors.

In Neil's illustrations, Dorothy appears quite different than she does in the film, and in several books. In the book Ozma of Oz, for instance, she's drawn with blonde hair, a white dress with a red sash and a red ribbon in her hair. She looks a bit more sophisticated, really, than the farm girl Dorothy we see in the original 1939 film.

His drawings make sophisticated use of line and color. In plates featuring Billina the chicken, for instance, she's oftentimes the same brilliant yellow as Dorothy's hair, with her red comb making her something of an imitation of Dorothy's yellow hair and red bow.

His mechanical creatures are a bit different than they appear in the film. Less organic and more mechanized looking, they tend to have thin arms with pronounced joints, many with friendly faces. The copper man, for instance, even sports a moustache and a round, plump appearance.

Neil's drawings of the characters oftentimes have a very regal appearance to them. The Scarecrow and Tin Man look far less human than they do in the film, for obvious reasons.

William Wallace Denslow

William Wallace Denslow was a colorful character who had a contentious relationship with Baum. The two split after a stage production of *The Wizard of Oz* in 1902. Denslow believed that he was entitled to a full share of the royalties.

Denslow's illustrations were far off from the appearance of the cast in *The Wizard of Oz*. His Cowardly Lion, for instance, is not a biped and looks basically like a lion complete with an expressive face. The Scarecrow is very doll like in appearance and the Tin Woodsman is very mechanical. Dorothy is plump, having a blue dress, socks and white shoes and appears to be quite a bit younger than she does in the film.

Denslow went on to illustrate other children's stories. He even incorporated some of Baum's characters into his own work. Not one for modesty, he eventually bought an island near Bermuda and subsequently declared himself king of it.

Denslow's Munchkins look very unlike what we see in the film. They wear conical hats and appear older, looking essentially like miniaturized adults. They look more or less like the gnomes that one often sees in popular culture today, with little of the childlike charm of the Lollipop Guild or Lullaby League.

Evelyn Copelman

While the drawings of Neil and Denslow are iconic, the 1939 film has likely contributed more to most people's understanding of what the characters in the Oz books look like than did either artist's illustrations. Evelyn Copelman was very much influenced by the films, and this shows in her work.

Today, most people, if asked, would likely draw the cast of characters from *The Wizard of Oz* roughly as they appear in the film. The first round of drawings that Copelman did were advertised as being related to the work that Denslow did, but most agree that this was not really the case. Her drawings depict the Tin Man, Dorothy and the Scarecrow looking much the same as they did in the film. The Cowardly Lion, however, does appear far less humanoid than he does in the film in many of Copelman's drawings.

Because Copelman had her drawings come out in the post-World War II era, they are the ones that most people how grew up with the annual showings of the film on television likely remember. There are differences, however, such as the Emerald City looking more medieval than the somewhat art deco look it has in the film. The colors, landscapes and sense of depth in the illustrations, however, are very developed and they take on something of a more realistic look during this period.

Copelman was born in 1919, being of the right age to have taken in the Oz novels as a child. She was the first artist after Denslow to make illustrations for the book *The Wonderful Wizard of Oz*, giving her a chance to really redefine the look in literature as much as it has been in film. Copelman died back in 2003.

Later Adaptations

Because Oz outlived its creator, the illustrations associated with it changed far beyond his vision or that of the early illustrators he worked with. There have been numerous different interpretations of Oz's landscapes and characters since, including graphic novels that were based in Oz.

Some of the artists who have worked on Oz and Oz-related illustrations include;

Dirk Gringhuis He was responsible for the illustrations for the book *The Hidden Valley of Oz* from 1951.

Dick Martin Martin completed the illustrations for several books that take place in the Oz universe and was very involved in the fandom community surrounding Baum's books. He served, for a while, as the editor of *The Baum Bugle*. He was also they president of The International Wizard of Oz fan club at one time and held various other posts within the organizations.

Eric Shanower Shanower writes novels and graphic novels set in the Oz universe. He has been doing so for decades, starting his career in the 1980s with the release of several comic books set in Oz. His novels have been adapted into graphic novels and he continues to produce books based in the world of Oz.

William Stout Stout has a long career as an album artist and as an artist working in other fields, including comics. He has illustrated two books set in the Oz universe.

The Biggest Difference

In Denslow and Neil's work, you'll see drawings that seem much more in line with the conventions of the early 1900s. Dorothy oftentimes appears with short hair in Neil's drawings and, in many regards, looks quite sophisticated and intelligent. His drawings invoke the modernity of Baum's work as compared to fairytales from the past very well, while still showing the fantasy elements in all of their glory.

In Denslow's work, there is more innocence and the characters appear a bit more childlike in terms of how they look and the obvious target audience for the drawings. As far as collecting art and books related to Oz, collectors generally prize the ones with Neil and Denslow's illustrations the most. Copelman, however, made very influential drawings in terms of how people perceive Dorothy and her group of friends, particularly given that those drawings fit so nicely with the image of those characters in the film.

As the films have evolved over time, the look of the characters has generally gotten darker. For instance, a look at the Wheelers in Neil's illustrations in *Ozma of Oz* as compared to how they appear in

Return to Oz reveals that, even though the general appearance is true to Neil, they're also far more frightening.

Oz has always been a land where dreams intertwine freely with nightmare imagery and, among the best illustrators, there's a great blend of nostalgia and the bizarre that makes great companions to the books.

Conclusion

The Munchkins in the *Wizard of Oz* only appear for a short time in the film, but their impact was significant. The actors and actresses that showed up represented a mix of seasoned performers, people who had only seen a stage from the audience seating position, and people who didn't even really know that there were other little people out there, much less that there was a place in Hollywood for them.

Over the years, little people who worked in Hollywood would have to face a lot of prejudice and many roles that were, quite frankly, insulting. As time went on, however, little people started to get better and better roles, including some of those who starred in the original *Wizard of Oz*.

Those roles would become more expansive, more challenging and more memorable as time went on. From material that really only put little people on screen so that the audience could look at them to roles in hugely successful productions such as *Seinfeld* and *Game of Thrones*, little people have started to assert themselves as being on an even keel as far as talent and capability are concerned and, increasingly, audiences don't seem to care about whether someone is a little person or not, as long as they can act well and make a story come alive.

That's where the Munchkins really shine in *The Wizard of Oz*. Rather than being regarded as part of a freak show, they're among the first people that Dorothy sees in Oz and are the first time the audience realizes that they're in a magical land. While the Technicolor's contrast with the sepia-toned Kansas also indicates this, the presence of the Munchkins symbolizes both Dorothy's entrance into the magical realm and the fact that there is good in the world that she's about to immerse herself in.

Over the years, the players who worked as Munchkins were able to captivate crowds at conventions and other events in ways that defined them forever as an integral part of the Oz mythology. *The Wizard of Oz* became one of the most American of all stories and they were a part of that; a significant part, no less.

Today, "dropping a house on someone", "there's no place like home", and other phrases from the film are words that everyone understands in terms of meaning and where they originally come from. Whenever you see little people on screen and realize how far they've come, remember that it all started at a spiral that began a Yellow Brick Road that led a little girl home, and on one of the most spectacular adventures ever put on film.

The 124 little people that answered a casting call and came from all over the world were part of the huge cast and crew that made that happen. They remained proud of it throughout their lives, and rightly so.

Sources Cited

http//www.imdb.com/title/tt0032138/trivia?ref_=tt_ql_2

http//www.people.com/people/article/0,,20120614,00.html

http//www.people.com/people/article/0,,20120614,00.html

http//hollywoodjournal.com/personal-journeys/how-game-of-thrones-changed-the-little-people/20130529/

wwaw.imdb.com/filmosearch?sort=year&explore=title_type&role=n m0546439&ref_=nm_ql_flmg_1

http//www.lpaonline.org/faq-#Definition

http//www.reuters.com/article/2007/11/21/us-munchkins-idUSN2062387820071121

http//www.themoneymasters.com/mm/the-wonderful-wizard-of-oz/

http//thewizardofoz.info/wiki/The_Movie_-_Cast

http//weird.answers.com/freaks-of-nature/fun-facts-about-the-wizard-of-oz-munchkins

http//www.thedailybeast.com/articles/2013/03/08/meet-ruth-duccinia-munchkin-from-the-wizard-of-oz.html

http//www.imdb.com/title/tt0032138/trivia?ref_=ttfc_ql_trv_1

http//www.imdb.com/title/tt0032138/trivia?ref_=ttfc_ql_trv_1

http//oz.wikia.com/wiki/The_Wizard_of_Oz_(1939)

http//www.westegg.com/inflation/infl.cgi

http//tvtropes.org/pmwiki/pmwiki.php/Main/ExecutiveMeddling

http//www.620wtmj.com/news/local/53036302.html

http//www.nytimes.com/movie/review?res=9B07EEDD1138EE3BB
C4052DFBE668382629EDE

http//badassdigest.com/2013/02/25/the-time-the-wicked-witch-of-
the-west-was-too-scary-for-sesame-street/

http//www.youtube.com/watch?v=u6kpcPD8bks

http//www.dailymail.co.uk/news/article-397458/The-secret-
salacious-world-Munchkins.html

http//www.warnersisters.com/index.php?option=com_content&view
=article&id=83the-wizard-of-oz-is-arguably-the-most-watched-
movie-ever-made&catid=8press&Itemid=9

http//www.imdb.com/title/tt0022913/plotsummary?ref_=tt_ql_6

http//www.snopes.com/movies/films/ozsuicide.asp

http//news.google.com/newspapers?nid=2245&dat=19971101&id=
K-40AAAAIBAJ&sjid=KyEGAAAAIBAJ&pg=5476,26169

http//www.mlive.com/entertainment/detroit/index.ssf/2013/03/photo
s_oz_the_great_and_powerf.html

http//www.imdb.com/name/nm0546439/?nmdp=1&ref_=nm_ql_5#f
ilmography

http//www.imdb.com/title/tt0083254/

http//www.rottentomatoes.com/m/under_the_rainbow/

http//oz.wikia.com/wiki/The_Wizard_of_Oz_(1939)

http//www.thedailyjournal.com/article/20090403/NEWS01/9040604
5/Pop-culture-history-Wizard-Oz-televised-1950s-

http//www.rifftrax.com/riff/wizard-oz

http//oz.wikia.com/wiki/Maps_of_Oz

http//oz.wikia.com/wiki/Maps_of_Oz?file=MapOfOz.jpg

http//www.funtrivia.com/en/subtopics/The-Wizard-of-Oz-Book-vs-Movie-300711.html

http//www.oz-stravaganza.com/home/history-of-l-frank-baum/mission-statement/news-releases/iwoc

http//www.oz-stravaganza.com/home/history-of-l-frank-baum/all-things-oz/l-frank-baum-munchkin-memorial

http//www.fearnet.com/news/news-article/annual-festival-takes-place-abandoned-wizard-oz-theme-park

http//www.visitwamego.com/Things-To-Do/Festivals-and-Events/OZtoberFest/

http//ozmuseum.com/about/default.htm

http//emanuellevy.com/comment/wizard-of-oz-cultural-impact-9/

http//voices.yahoo.com/political-symbolism-the-wizard-oz-book-movie-561662.html?cat=40

http//news.bbc.co.uk/2/hi/uk_news/magazine/7933175.stm

http//ozconinternational.com/about-us.html

http//articles.latimes.com/1988-03-13/entertainment/ca-1511_1_ruby-slipper

http//www.ebay.com/itm/Original-1939-MGM-Screen-Worn-MUNCHKIN-COSTUME-From-THE-WIZARD-OF-OZ-/131126621629?nma=true&si=nixqgPfzuncVyE8v9k5aws8482s%253D&orig_cvip=true&rt=nc&_trksid=p2047675.l2557

http//www.costumersguide.com/oz_review4.shtml

http//www.julienslive.com/view-auctions/catalog/id/55/lot/18161/

http//www.youtube.com/watch?v=A5s8LURnmpc

http//www.usatoday.com/story/travel/destinations/2013/10/18/wizard-of-oz-props-collection-exhibit-display/3007297/

http//www.smithsonianmag.com/arts-culture/frank-baum-the-man-behind-the-curtain-32476330/?no-ist

http//oz.wikia.com/wiki/Evelyn_Copelman

http//www.imdb.com/name/nm0178673/

http//www.mesothelioma.com/asbestos-exposure/products/fake-snow/

http//tvtropes.org/pmwiki/pmwiki.php/NightmareFuel/TheWizardOf Oz

43084568R00079

Made in the USA
San Bernardino, CA
14 December 2016